How to
RIGHT
a dog gone
WRONG

Other books by Pamela S. Dennison:

The Complete Idiot's Guide to Positive Dog Training, Alpha Books

Bringing Light to Shadow: A Dog Trainer's Diary, Dogwise Publishing

Coming Soon: *Click Your Way to Rally Obedience,* Alpine Publications

How to RIGHT a dog gone WRONG

A Road Map for Rehabilitating Aggressive Dogs

Pamela S. Dennison

Alpine
Blue Ribbon Books
Loveland, Colorado

Cataloging in Publication Data

Dennison, Pamela
   How to right a dog gone wrong : a road map for rehabilitating aggressive dogs
   / Pamela S. Dennison
      p. cm.   Includes index
      ISBN 1-57779-075-8
1. Dogs—Training. 2. Dogs—Behavior. 3. Aggressive behavior in animals
1. Title
   SF431.D446 2005   2005048004
      636.7'0835 22

The information contained in this book is complete and accurate to the best of our knowledge. All recommendations are made without guarantee on the part of the author or Alpine Publications, Inc. The author and publisher disclaim any liability with the use of this information.

This book is available at special quantity discounts for breeders and for club promotions, premiums, or educational use. Write for details.

For the sake of simplicity, the terms "he" or "she" are sometimes used to identify an animal or person. These are used in the generic sense only. No discrimination of any kind is intended toward either sex.

Many manufacturers secure trademark rights for their products. When Alpine Publications is aware of a trademark claim, we identify the product name by using initial capital letters.

Cover and text design and layout : Laura Newport
Cover photo: Meg Irizarry
Editing: Deborah Helmers

 2 3 4 5 6 7 8 9 0

Printed in the United States of America.

TABLE OF CONTENTS

❧ *Aggression: What is it used for?* ❧ *What's in a label?*
❧ *Identifying your dog's issues* ❧ *What your dog is trying to tell you*
❧ *Early indicators of aggression*

❧ **Human-caused aggression** ❧ *Support of aggressive behaviors*
❧ *Passivity or poor timing* ❧ *Punishment*
❧ *Leashes, tie-outs, prong collars, choke collars and head halters*
❧ *Electric fences* ❧ *Windows, barriers and teasing animals or humans*
❧ *Lack of proper exercise and enough safe chances to just be a dog*
❧ *Lack of basic training* ❧ *Accidental reinforcement of dominant or dog-aggressive behavior* ❧ **Medical problems**

❧ **Facing the facts** ❧ *Recognizing aggression* ❧ *Denial*
❧ *Expectations versus reality* ❧ **Peer pressure** ❧ **Self-sabotage**
❧ **Reactions of your dog to your stress** ❧ **Controlling your own stress**
❧ *Belly breathing* ❧ *Positive mental imagery* ❧ *Your safe place*
❧ **Keep your eye on the goal**

❧ **Training to prevent aggression** ❧ **Debunking the alpha dog model**
❧ **Continuing his education** ❧ *Socialize appropriately*
❧ *Socialize your pup at his own pace* ❧ *Attend a formal class*
❧ **Primary caretaking: an adult responsibility**
❧ **Dealing with fear periods** ❧ **Basic lessons every puppy must learn**
❧ *Accepting Handling* ❧ *Sensible house training* ❧ *Appropriate use of mouth*
❧ *Sharing* ❧ **Protecting your dog** ❧ *Socialize with appropriate dogs*

Dedicated to the dogs that need our help
and to the people willing to help them.

And to Ellen Griffith, the bravest person I know,
and her Beagle, Moni.

FOREWORD

It's always tragic when a young, otherwise healthy dog is euthanized for behavior reasons. Sadly, that happens to thousands of dogs in this country every year, often because of aggression. It's especially tragic because in the majority of cases behavior problems, even aggressive behavior, can be modified. More importantly, aggression can be prevented.

All dogs bite – it's a normal behavior for canids. Aggression is a natural response to stress, fear, and anxiety, important for survival in the wild. However, it's becoming an increasingly unacceptable behavior for dogs who live in a human world. While dog-related human fatalities are exceedingly rare, especially when compared to statistics on deaths by other more mundane causes such as auto accidents and child abuse, they are always sensational – and sensationalized. Maulings are also relatively uncommon, but garden-variety punctures and lacerations are common and on the rise. In a society increasingly uneducated about and intolerant of normal dog behavior, even a garden-variety bite gets dog and dog owner into serious trouble.

In days gone by, when Fido bit Johnny, Mom was likely to say, "What did you do to make the dog bite you, Johnny?" Times have changed. Today, Fido's declared a dangerous dog, Johnny's parents sue Fido's owner, and Fido's owner loses his homeowner's insurance.

If you share your life with a canine companion or are thinking of adding one to your family, you owe it to that dog to learn how to prevent aggressive behaviors from occurring, how to recognize early signs of inappropriate aggressive behavior, and how to take immediate, appropriate and effective steps to reprogram a dog's aggressive responses should they occur. Experienced dog trainer, and owner of Shadow, a rehabilitated once-aggressive Border Collie, author Pam Dennison is here to help you do just that. In these pages you'll find sound advice about proper socialization and training to prevent aggression, as well as detailed instructions to help you modify your dog's already-aggressive behavior.

So what are you waiting for? Turn the page and start reading. It could save your dog's life.

Pat Miller
Certified Pet Dog Trainer, Certified Dog Behavior Consultant
Author of "The Power of Positive Dog Training," and "Positive Perspectives"
Owner, Peaceable Paws, LLC, Hagerstown, MD

ACKNOWLEDGMENTS

My everlasting appreciation goes to Jane Killion, Ted Turner, John and Cynthia Palmer, Meg Irizarry, Eve Cutter, Suzanne Loftus, Jill Zimmer, Deb Manheim, Terri Bright and Virginia Wind for their support in helping me coalesce my thoughts, critiquing portions of the manuscript and helping to make me a better trainer, writer and person.

To Robert Sapolsky, who gave up some of his precious time to help me understand a topic that doesn't come naturally to me and was quite gracious and patient when I kept getting it wrong. He didn't give up until I got it right!

To all of my students and their dogs: Stacy, Anna, Audrey, Pat, Dave, Sue, Gerry, Allison, Bryn, Rebecca, Ethel, Ellen, Andrea, Beth, Bob, Jen and more, many of whom grace this book with their stories and pictures. They have all taught me so much.

To my agent and friend Jacky Sach, for her ever-present faith in me.

And to Shadow (Ewe Are Beyond a Shadow of a Doubt, CGC, R1MCL, R2CL, NA), who started it all.

INTRODUCTION

There is no greater joy in the world than working with and seeing progress from your aggressive dog. The process of retraining an aggressive dog is not quick or easy. The dedication and patience you put in will pay off, not just in improved behavior from your dog, but in incredible self-esteem and sense of accomplishment for yourself. Being able to take your dog to places once fraught with danger is an enabling and life-changing experience. Stopping inappropriate behaviors before they get out of hand is even better!

That's how it happened for me. I adopted a one-year-old Border Collie that turned out to be human-aggressive. After having Shadow for only two weeks, I was ready to send him back to the rescue group, but hesitated to do so because I knew he would have to be euthanized. I happened to be talking to one of my students and I mentioned that I was thinking about sending Shadow back. She said, "No—this is terrific! You can learn how to handle him and teach us!" As soon as she said that, it hit me: "If I give up on this dog, how can I expect my students not to give up on theirs?" I decided to keep him and work on his issues. Because of the time I have spent with him, he is now able to compete successfully in agility and Rally obedience, and I continue to train for many other dog sports. I have been able to take the positive principles that led to Shadow's accomplishments and use them to guide owners of other aggressive dogs, and I have seen many of those dogs "graduate" into a more normal lifestyle. To witness the growing expertise and confidence of these students, both human and canine, gives me goose bumps!

There are no magic potions, special tools, complicated training methods or mysterious mumbo-jumbo gimmicks I can give to you to work with your aggressive dog. However, I will show you proven, solid, easy-to-understand basics, and lay out the science you'll need for the process. Understanding your best, albeit complex, friend, is not as difficult as you think. The simpler the process is kept, the better off you and your dog will be. The basics, pure and simple—classical conditioning, operant conditioning, counterconditioning and systematic desensitization—are what you'll find here. By understanding and utilizing positive principles, you will better be able to find a solution to your dog's problems as well as avoid issues in the future. I also discuss how your own reactions very often can have a strong effect on your dog's behavior.

I have laid out these terms and behaviors in a user-friendly manner and they will soon be as familiar and as comfortable as your favorite pair of shoes. Each behavior and context is broken down into small steps for you, just as you will learn to break down each scenario for your dog. If your dog's issues don't exactly match the examples here—perhaps your dog isn't wildly aggressive, but you have lived through a few incidents that you aren't happy about—you should have no problem adjusting the exercises listed in this book to fit your needs.

If, when reading these pages, you see things that you may have done incorrectly, try not to kick yourself. Learn from your mistakes, adjust your mind-set, help your dog and move on. Without a clear plan of action, owning an aggressive dog can be depressing, frightening, disheartening, debilitating, embarrassing and intensely frustrating. This book is designed to give you that plan of action and with it, hope.

Pamela S. Dennison
May 2005

Is Your Dog Aggressive?

AGGRESSION: WHAT IS IT USED FOR?

It is important to understand that aggression is a *normal* behavior. Aggression helps every species remain alive, procreate and keep safe from real or perceived danger. An aggressive act is scary to watch and frequently can be misinterpreted, especially if the use and need for it aren't understood. Most acts of aggression, no matter how frightening to watch, are actually not meant to do harm but, rather, to warn away danger or a competitor.

Every species must have ritualized methods of avoiding severe, "fight to the death" aggression; otherwise, the species would quickly become extinct. For instance, many wild animals—lions, rams, wild horses, bears, and even squirrels—have specific ways of "duking it out," while actually leaving opponents intact with no real damage done. As Konrad Lorenz says in his book *On Aggression,* "Aggression of so many animals toward members of their own species is in no way detrimental to the species, but, on the contrary, is essential for its preservation."

We humans also have a need to exhibit aggression, although it isn't necessary to our survival in this day and age. In *Coercion and Its Fallout,* Murray Sidman points out that "prohibited by social custom and law from striking each other, we watch football, wrestling or boxing; bridge, chess and checkers too, are socially approved forms of competitive aggression."

Like us, our companion dogs no longer need to fight to stay alive— we care for them, feed and clothe them, take care of their medical needs, and give them a warm place by the fire and a soft place at the foot of our beds. However, the instinctual need for aggression still remains within them, and when it surfaces, it frightens us. We try to "remedy" this scary but perfectly normal stuff, and in our ignorance, we may blunder and botch it so that our dogs do, sometimes, fight to the death.

For our dogs to successfully co-exist with us in our human society, we must teach them that aggressive behaviors are no longer essential; we must channel those behaviors into, as Sidman says, "socially approved forms of competitive aggression." For example, we can concentrate the dogs' energies toward sports such as agility, tracking, sheepherding, musical Freestyle, Rally obedience and many other dog sports. We also must make sure that we do not unwittingly intensify or even cause the very aggression we are trying to control. In the next few chapters we will explore the ways that humans cause aggression in dogs, since that is the cause we can most easily control. Just as the dog must learn about our world, we must learn about his.

WHAT'S IN A LABEL?

There seems to be a big push lately for labels for each type of aggression: dominance aggression, fear aggression, idiopathic aggression (which actually means that the person giving out the "diagnosis" has no idea as to its cause), inter-animal aggression, pain aggression, play aggression, predatory aggression, territorial aggression, food-related aggression, maternal aggression, and possessive aggression. The label itself often becomes too complicated and confusing—it can actually hinder and bog down effective treatment. Additionally, once the "diagnosis" is given, an owner may come to feel that the behavior can't be changed and give up completely, either euthanizing the dog or dumping him in an unsuspecting shelter.

Although labels may be important to an owner on some level (knowing the name of the "disease" may make a person feel better), what is really more important—in fact, what is crucial—is not the label itself, but knowing exactly what triggers the dog to aggress. This may be people, dogs or other animals, the food bowl, tactile stimulation (touching), or the perceived need to guard objects, territory or people. It is thus much easier simply to define what a dog reacts to, than to spend time seeking out the fancy words that most of us have to look up in the dictionary.

The information you will receive in this book will help you and your dog, no matter what his issues are. Yes, your dog is special, but the ways and means for the systematic desensitization process—the process that will transform your dog's behavior in the face of his own particular scary bad things—are all the same.

IDENTIFYING YOUR DOG'S ISSUES

Many reactive or aggressive dogs have more than one issue. You will need to recognize and define each one as a separate entity. To start the systematic desensitization process, you'll have to write down, in exacting detail, a list of each thing your dog is afraid of, for fear is where aggression begins. The following are some examples of different things human-aggressive dogs may find scary:

- Eye contact from a stranger
- Body parts, hands, legs or feet moving in weird—or even normal— ways (such as reaching out to pet the dog or leaning over)
- Loud sounds from people
- People coming up from behind
- Large groups of people
- Small groups of people
- Men (especially those with facial hair or wearing hats)
- Women
- Kids on bikes or skateboards
- People in a training building (such as during a group class)

The following are some examples of different things a dog-aggressive dog may find scary:

- Another dog looking at him
- Another dog running or chasing something, such as a ball or toy, or even running agility
- Another dog barking, lunging or pulling on leash
- Large groups of other dogs
- Small groups of other dogs
- Dogs getting too close, either outside or inside a training building

❧ Certain breeds of dogs

❧ Certain sexes of dogs

Your dog may have other issues, such as:

❧ Difficulty in accepting touch, or any other grooming/handling issues

❧ Aggressing when people, dogs, cars, or kids go past your fence line

❧ Being afraid of certain inanimate objects

❧ Aggressing on leash although fine off leash (more commonly called "leash aggression")

Suppose your dog is human-aggressive, will not accept grooming (even from you), and is afraid of bulky winter coats.

To be able to work on these problems, you need to break them down even more. Ask yourself exactly how and in what situations is he aggressive toward people? Is the problem with large groups of people or a single person? Does it involve direct contact (touching), direct eye contact, fast-moving people, kids, loud noises or moving body parts? Is he aggressive off leash, on leash, through a fence, up close (define how close), at home, away from home, far away (define far away), or toward people who come out of nowhere? What part of grooming is he sensitive about—nails, shaving, ear cleaning, scissoring around his face or legs, or hind end brushing? Is he afraid of you leaning over him or of being on the table or on the floor? Is he afraid of men, women or kids wearing that bulky coat? Does he aggress even if familiar people that he likes wear the coat?

Suppose your dog is dog-aggressive and also afraid of the garbage truck and flags. Let's break this scenario down. Is he aggressive toward one dog or many dogs? At what distance? Does he aggress at neutered or intact male dogs, spayed or intact female dogs, or puppies? Is he more aggressive when he is on leash or off leash, behind a barrier, in his own yard or away from home, when dogs walk straight up to him or when they come from behind him, or towards any particular breed(s) of dogs? What is the other dog doing when your dog reacts? Is he playing, lunging, barking, chasing or minding his own business? Regarding the other issues, is your dog afraid of the noise, sight or movement of the garbage truck or the sound or movement of the flag?

The catch-all terms "human-aggressive" or "dog-aggressive" are extremely general. You can uncover much more specific and useful information simply by breaking each issue down into its exact components. You must do this; otherwise, you may be inadvertently setting your dog up to aggress because you haven't defined and recognized each distinct problem in its entirety. In order to cope with your dog in the real world, you must have an intimate understanding of his specific triggers. It will be helpful for you to set up a log sheet like this:

Date:_____

Things my dog aggresses at: ___Men ___Women ___Kids (define—ages, walking, running, on bikes or skateboards, swimming, playing)_____
___Men in hats ___Men with beards ___One person alone ___Groups of people
___Eye contact from strangers ___ Moving body parts ___Direct contact
___Grooming (define)_____
___People walking ___People running/jogging ___People coming up from behind
___Mail or UPS person ___ People on the other side of a fence or barrier
Other _____
___Direct eye contact from a dog ___Certain breed(s) of dogs (list)_____
___Male dogs (intact/neutered) ___Female dogs (intact/spayed) ___Dogs running
___Dogs walking ___Dogs playing ___Dogs coming up to the crate
___Dogs approaching head on ___Dogs sniffing his hind end ___On leash
___Off leash ___Puppies
Other_____
Inanimate objects: ___Coats ___Sunglasses ___Hats ___Gloves ___Boots
___Umbrellas ___Playground equipment ___Stuffed animals ___Drainpipes
___Manhole covers ___Papers blowing in the wind ___Loud noises ___Trucks
___Water (bath, lake or river) ___Gravel ___Ice ___Pots and pans dropping
___Thunder___Shopping carts ___Loud music
Other_____

There is a blank form in Appendix 1 that you can copy and use. I recommend you fill it out and date it, and then review and redo the form every six months. The progress you see will help you keep focused in your training program.

Once you have examined and written down the ins and outs of your dog's issues, you can start addressing them. You will incorporate certain basic foundation behaviors into new circumstances or contexts, being careful not to stress your dog as you do so. You will see progress if you move slowly through this desensitization process.

WHAT YOUR DOG IS TRYING TO TELL YOU

An important part of the desensitization process is to fully understand your dog's body language so that you can start a session while he is calm and end a session before he aggresses. The most noteworthy research in this field has been done by Turid Rugaas, a dog trainer from Norway. Through incredible observational skills, Ms. Rugaas has been instrumental in unraveling the mystery of the signals that dogs use to communicate, providing thousands of owners and trainers a more accurate understanding of dog behavior. If you are alert and attentive to what your dog is telling you, it is much easier to help him effectively. For in-depth reading and viewing, Ms. Rugaas' book and video are listed in Appendix 2 and are "must haves" for every dog owner's library.

> You must begin training sessions while your dog is calm and end them before he becomes stressed.

The short list of stress signals a dog will give off (as long as he hasn't been punished for them in the past) is as follows:

- **Mild**—Head turning away, eyes turning away, blinking, panting, yawning, sniffing, drooling, lip licking, arcing (or curving), raising a paw (as if to "shake").

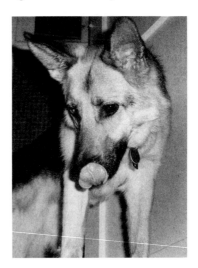

Lip licking. Photo by M. Irizarry.

This dog is staring at another dog; her nose is just starting to be pushed forward and her face is showing stress wrinkles. Photo by M. Irizarry.

* **Medium**—Eating grass, eating poop, short attention span, wagging tail frantically, spinning/circling, drinking water, lip lifting, staring.

The same dog is now giving off more active "go away" behaviors—teeth showing, face pushed forward, ears back. Photo by M. Irizarry.

* **Hot**—Slow, reluctant behaviors, stopping or freezing (in an awkward position), lying down, sitting, shivering (as if cold), shaking (as if shaking off water), sweaty paws, raised temperature (ears can get hot and a male dog may stick his penis out of the sheath in an attempt to cool himself down), scratching, sneezing, baring teeth.
* **Bring out the fire extinguisher**—Chewing, digging, diarrhea, loss of appetite (won't take treats), turning body completely away, raising hackles, biting the leash, "stress" shedding and dandruff, hyperbehavior, self-mutilation, whining, barking, howling, growling, baring teeth, aggressing.

If you see any of the signs listed above, you'll need to back off in distance, duration or intensity with regard to whatever stimulus is provoking your dog. Ignoring the early signs of stress might just result in your dog's behavior escalating—you will have missed the opportunity to redirect him to a positive activity. If you can recognize your dog's stress signs at the earliest possible moment, when they are mild, you can end the session and rethink your criteria before your dog explodes.

Annie had a punishment-based training background. She wanted to learn how to do Rally obedience using positive techniques and came to my class. Her Australian Shepherd, Bonnie, was starting to aggress at certain people and was very nervous in general, presenting such signals as stress shedding, head turning, lip licking, yawning, and slow, reluctant behaviors. I noticed that Bonnie had huge patches on her body with no fur and asked if she had recently been spayed. Annie told me that Bonnie had always chewed on herself. After six weeks of training and a greater understanding of how to read her dog, Annie was able to make better training decisions and told me that Bonnie had stopped the self-mutilating behavior completely. After twelve weeks of classes, Bonnie has stopped aggressing at people as well.

You must be observant and sensitive to evidence that your dog is experiencing stress. Since stress can manifest itself in various ways from dog to dog, I call these your dog's personal stress signals; however, a general tightening of posture or stiffening of muscles is a fairly reliable barometer of increasing tension. You may see a stiffening of the tail or ears; a change in the appearance of the muzzle and mouth; a heightened, more intense look in the eyes, including enlarged pupils; puffed cheeks and short, explosive breaths; foaming at the mouth (significantly different from drooling); and a noticeable tightness of the mouth when taking food.

When working with my dog Shadow on, for example, the stand for exam, I am so cognizant of his stress signs that I know when I can push the session and when I should back off. When I started to work on this behavior, if his pupils got large, his eyes changed shape, he turned his head away or his mouth got tight, I ended the session. Now I end the session way before he ever even thinks about showing these signs.

EARLY INDICATORS OF AGGRESSION

There are many early warning signs that your dog is becoming aggressive. Dogs don't just wake up one morning and say to themselves, "I think I'll be aggressive from now on." It usually has been building and escalating for quite some time, until—voilá!—you have full-blown aggression. You think he is demented, deranged, derailed, insane because the slightest things set him off into an aggressive display. You are at a loss as to what to do to "fix" your dog and may have gotten advice that, when followed, resulted in a problem much worse than what you started with.

It takes a keen eye and clear understanding of what is and is not appropriate dog behavior to recognize the warning signs that your dog is becoming aggressive. Knowing these signals will help you understand your dog's behavior in a different way and will allow you to make positive training choices before the situation gets out of hand.

When Alice and Barry were running into typical adolescent issues with their Australian Cattle Dog, Peter, they were told to alpha roll and scruff shake him to stop the inappropriate behaviors. Although this treatment did suppress certain of the annoying things he was doing, because of the negative associations now connected with handling, it also created a dog that will no longer allow

Signs that your dog is starting to develop some aggression issues can include any or all of the following:

❖ He won't allow you or other people to handle him.

❖ He tries to bite you to get you to stop petting or brushing him.

❖ He bites and nips excessively while playing.

❖ His reactivity (barking, lunging, backing away, growling) to dogs, adults or children is out of proportion to the situation and he can't calm down within a few seconds.

❖ He doesn't respond well to change and startles at any new thing he sees or hears.

❖ He freaks out when someone comes to the door and isn't able to calm down within a few seconds.

❖ Any new person or dog he sees causes him to go crazy.

❖ He has been kicked out of obedience class because he is disruptive to the other students.

❖ He guards objects—food and water bowls, toys, rooms, his crate, furniture and, possibly, even you.

his owners to touch him in any way. Strangers, however, do not come with the same bad associations and can do anything to Peter and he enjoys it—from petting to grooming.

Many puppies go through these kinds of issues to some degree, but that does not mean serious problems are inevitable. If the behaviors are addressed properly as soon as they start, they will not become serious issues later on.

POINTS TO PONDER

- *Aggression is normal. A dog's natural aggressive instinct must be channeled into socially acceptable behaviors.*
- *In order to help your dog, you must first identify in detail his own unique issues.*
- *Retraining involves being able to read your dog's stress signals and stop a session before he becomes stressed.*

Causes of Aggression

HUMAN-CAUSED AGGRESSION

There are many things that humans unwittingly do to promote inappropriate aggression in their dogs, and we will be discussing them in this chapter. Many times, well-meaning owners will adopt a training strategy that is intended to remedy a problem, but in reality makes the aggression worse. It will help you when you are retraining your dog if you have a clear understanding of how and why these training strategies don't work and may actually create more serious problems. Once training errors are recognized and understood, positive solutions that *do* work will be waiting for you.

Support of Aggressive Behaviors

Very often people *want* their dogs to be aggressive. It seems to give some individuals a feeling of power to be in "control" of an aggressive dog. Many people themselves possess aggressive tendencies and so they encourage the dog to take on their own personas. Some people want an "attack" dog because they are afraid: "Good dog, you protected me!" Oddly enough, these people often get angry at their dog when he cannot distinguish between a malevolent stranger and a friendly one. The dog knows only "us," meaning his family, and "them," meaning every other person in the entire world. If encouraged to aggress at "them," he is going to aggress at every single person he meets—which may include the neighbor's four-year-old child who just happens to wander into the yard.

HUMAN CONDITIONS AND BEHAVIORS THAT REINFORCE AGGRESSION OR STRESS

- Supporting aggressive behaviors
- Having poor timing or being passive in the face of aggression
- Punishing the dog
- Using tie-outs, prong collars, choke collars, no-bark collars, citronella collars, and head halters
- Using electric fences
- Exposing the dog to frustrating barriers, such as windows and fences and allowing other animals or people to tease the dog
- Not providing proper exercise and sufficient safe chances to be a dog
- Not providing basic training
- Accidentally reinforcing dominant or aggressive behavior

What many people do not understand is that an aggressive dog is not protecting *them*—he is protecting *himself* (or possibly his person as a valued resource). In fact, K9 Police and protection dogs are chosen not for their aggressive tendencies, but for their solid temperaments.

Passivity or Poor Timing

For whatever reason, some people put a dog in a position to aggress and then just stand passively by and watch the dog freak out. They may then drag the dog away, but it is too late at that point—the dog has already been afraid and practiced the aggression. Truly, "an ounce of prevention is worth a pound of cure"—simply standing around while bad stuff happens creates many problems; however, leaving the scene as soon as possible will cut your training losses. If you don't leave quickly, you'll discover the validity of another wise saying, "practice makes perfect." Unfortunately, the thing that the dog is practicing and making perfect is aggression.

Ideally, you would never let your dog get into a situation where he might aggress. Most dogs aggress because they are afraid and they want to get away from the "scary" person or dog; thus, moving the dog away actually reinforces him for aggressing. However, once you have messed up or been legitimately caught off guard, you are in a lose-lose situation and you have to make choices. If you are in the thick of a bad situation, getting out of Dodge will do much less damage to your dog than letting him stay there and aggress!

I have seen people praise their dog for aggressing, thinking that praise will stop the behavior. "Good dog" is said repeatedly in the hope that the dog will magically become a good dog. Comforting the dog is also used in an attempt to stop the behavior by supposedly calming him down. "It's okay, silly dog—it's only Aunt Eugenia!" *(pet, pet, pat, pat).* In reality, the comfort reinforces the dog for his aggressive behavior.

Your dog may be pushy and domineering with you or others, having trained you to respond with speed and alacrity to his slightest whim. He has *learned* that excessive barking for attention, whining, mouthing and stealing objects makes you jump through hoops to do his bidding. Any attempt at changing his behavior may cause the aggression in your dog to escalate because you aren't playing by his rules anymore.

Poor timing can also be a problem in training. In the past, you may have actually inadvertently reinforced your dog for aggressing. Let's say you are taking your dog for a walk. He aggresses at something; you call him back to you and then instantly feed him some treats, thinking you reinforced him for the recall. In fact, you rewarded him for aggressing because your timing was off. You have created a pattern or chain—lunge, return, eat—lunge, return, eat—cha, cha, cha. Had you called the dog, asked him to do three behaviors (such as sit, down and settle), putting some time and other behaviors in between the treats and aggressing, and *then* reinforced your dog, you would then have been reinforcing the correct behavior—paying attention to you.

If you have inadvertently reinforced your dog's aggression by allowing him to be in charge, it doesn't mean that you can't change his behavior and put yourself back in the picture as the "benevolent leader." What it does mean is that you have to learn to be smarter, more patient and more manipulative (in a positive way) than he is.

Many people are either passive or oblivious regarding their dog's problems. They let their dog run off leash in public places to wreak havoc with joggers, hikers, kids and dogs. Don't let this be you.

At one of my aggressive dog classes, we were all taking a walk together on a trail. All of a sudden, two loose dogs rushed up to us, with no owner in sight. The two loose dogs ganged up on Bonnie, who is dog-aggressive. Thankfully, nothing terrible happened to her and one of the other students grabbed the loose dogs by the collar and led them away. The response from the owner of the loose dogs? "I can let my dogs off leash if I want to." Because Bonnie is far along in her training, she was able to recover within a few minutes.

Punishment

Some people yell at their dogs for aggressing—perhaps they are embarrassed or think that is what one should do when a dog exhibits inappropriate behaviors. The dog is already aroused, and yelling, yanking or hitting only puts him into arousal overload. Any punishment, even mild verbal scolding, can increase fear and stress. Furthermore, by pairing the pain or fear of punishment with the "scary" person or dog, the dog's fear that the "scary" thing is a genuine threat is confirmed.

Another area where many owners use punishment in a misguided fashion is when they punish a dog for growling or giving other warning signals on the theory that they can nip aggression in the bud by showing the dog "who's boss." Let's look at this carefully, from a behavioral standpoint, not from an emotional "I'll teach him not to aggress by punishing him" view. Your dog growls and you punish him. He stops growling, but did it rectify the *reason* that he was growling in the first place? Did it help him overcome his fear of the person, dog or object? Did it teach him that people/dogs are the best things since sliced bread? Or, rather, did it teach him that people/dogs are, in fact, dangerous? The next time he is confronted with that stimulus, he may suppress the growl—since it got him into big trouble the last time—and go directly to biting.

Dogs that have been punished for showing any overt signs of fear—whining, growling, low rumbles, teeth bared, hackles raised—will learn to mask these signs to avoid punishment. However, since they then have no way to warn off others, they have no option but to go directly to biting once they reach total overload. These are the dogs that bite "out of nowhere."

When I used to groom, there were times, especially when clipping toenails, that a dog would growl at me. I would say, "Thank you!" and then get down on my knees and thank his owner for not punishing him for growling. Why was I so grateful? Because the dog was able to warn me he was stressed and did not go directly to biting.

Your best bet is to not put your dog in a position where he feels he has to growl to warn you or others away. If he does growl, reinforce him the *first* time by walking away, and view this as a training wake-up call.

Then get to work and train the dog to accept whatever it was he was uncomfortable with.

There are observable results of using punishment as a method for controlling behavior. Punishment can lead to and cause a variety of negative behaviors, including aggression. Punish a dog and he will do one or more of the following:

- Try to escape the punishment (or the person doling out the punishment), learn to avoid it or embrace aggressive strategies to cope with it. Using punishment puts the dog into a flight-or-fight response.

- Redirect his aggression to you, or anything else the dog perceives as being more vulnerable (the sofa, small kids, smaller dogs, the leash), often in *seemingly* unrelated contexts. This describes what is often called displacement or redirected anxiety or aggression. We humans do the same things—our employer yells at us and we can't yell back because we need the job. So we aggress at anyone it is *safe* to aggress at—co-workers, drivers on the way home, family members.

- Learn to suppress the aggressive behavior for a short span, but over time become desensitized to the punishment—that is, the punishment will have to be repeated or increased in severity to stop the aggression. When using punishment to maintain good behaviors, the punishment has to increase in intensity.

- Become "compliant"; however, even if he "complies," the potential bad associations that the dog may learn are too negative to create a long-term beneficial outcome. For example, let's say that you hit your dog for jumping on people coming to the door. Your dog may now make the association that people coming to the door cause him pain and are dangerous—he might escalate from jumping on them to biting them. Or suppose your dog runs away and when you finally get him back, you punish him. Do you think he will understand that you punished him for running away? No. You have now just punished the "come"! Do you think he will come to you promptly the next time he gets loose?

Punishment *does* suppress behavior; it does not, however, eliminate it. It will come back in a minute, a day, a week or a month, and you may very well end up with a host of other problems that at first may not appear to be related to the punishment. For instance, punish your dog for eating your shoes and he may start eating the couch. The main problem with suppression is that it *looks* like the punishment works, when in reality it does not—not in the long run.

So what constitutes punishment? Punishment can be a yell, a slap, a jerk on the leash; certain phrases like "wrong" or "uh-uh"; shake cans filled with pennies; spray bottles; citronella, prong, choke and shock collars; and even human mood swings.

> When you use positive training, you teach alternate behaviors to replace the aggressive ones. Thus, you bring about an active, long-term solution, not a suppression of the problem. When you use punishment, you do not teach other behavioral strategies for the dog; you simply leave a void. The dog may stop aggressing for the moment, but he doesn't know what to do to instead. Have no doubt that he will fill in the void with something—and if you don't teach him an acceptable behavior, he may fill the void with an aggressive one.

People may misinterpret normal dog play as aggression and run in yelling and screaming to supposedly stop the "fight." The fact is that dogs don't play Parcheesi—they bite, body slam, bark and growl, so what we perceive as aggressive is actually normal. When we intervene in a hysterical way, the play may quickly escalate into a real fight, usually ending with more damage to the dog and human than the dog meant to do.

Were this a real fight, your physical punishment would only justify the dog's reaction to that stimulus (bad things happen around this scary thing—must drive this scary and bad thing away). If he is physically or verbally punished, your dog may become more afraid and aggressive toward the particular stimulus.

You *must* give up using punishment as a method for controlling aggressive behavior. The *Merck Veterinary Manual,* in "Behavioral Problems Associated with Canine Aggression," states: "Almost without exception, physical punishment, including the use of prong collars and electric shock collars, alpha rolls, and dominance downs can make an already aggressive dog worse. Owners should be discouraged from using these techniques...."

A woman came to me with a mildly dog-reactive dog. I worked with her for two lessons and she never came back for more training. She could not see the benefit of positive methods and went back to punishing her dog for reacting. I saw her again about a year later. Her dog was now violently aggressive, and not only to dogs, but toward people as well—he had sent at least one person to the hospital. The especially sad part was that this woman still did not see the correlation between the increased punishment and the increased aggression.

Leashes, Tie-Outs, Prong Collars, Choke Collars and Head Halters

Although meant to protect dogs, leashes can often exacerbate aggression. The dog knows he can't move away from danger and thus keep himself safe. A dog at the end of a tight leash often gives off more aggressive behavior signals than he probably intends. A tight leash puts the dog's opposition reflex (his instinctive reaction to move against anything that is pushing or pulling against him, i.e., the body's natural tendency to maintain balance) into high gear. For example, when you push a dog away that is jumping on you, he jumps even more.

Another dog seeing a dog frantically pulling on leash may read that behavior as aggressive. At the same time, the dog that is pulling now not only has increased his excitement for the dog or human out of reach, but also has lost interest in his owner. With an aggressive dog, this can mean lunging, growling and barking in a wild frenzy. The tight leash can also be seen as a punishment because it hurts the dog, adding more problems into the mix.

If a dog is afraid, most of the time other dogs will recognize that fear and avoid doing anything to increase it, such as approaching the scared dog. Humans, on the other hand, either are often unaware of what behaviors indicate fear or fail to pay attention to them. Not only do people fail to recognize fear behaviors, but they frequently mislabel them as stubbornness, hardheadedness or dominance, which results in very inappropriate human reactions that can have disastrous results.

I have seen people approach and try to pet dogs that were viciously aggressing at them. They seemed to be completely oblivious to the dog's behavior. When asked to stop their approach, they say, "Oh, it's okay—I love dogs." They do not seem to realize that continuing to approach a fearful dog will only increase his fear, and the dog will most likely attempt to run away or growl, air snap, or bite the person or dog who comes too close.

Prong and choke collars as well as head halters can also have an adverse effect on your dog. Picture that same dog with the tight leash on a prong or choke collar; the prongs are digging into his neck or the choke chain is choking him. With head halters, the dog's head is wrenched around (possibly causing neck and spinal damage), *forcing* him into a vulnerable position. In addition, head halters restrict normal head and body movements and thus compromise natural communication signals. Such "training" aids lead the dog to associate pain with the object he is lunging or aggressing at—not a good start to the desensitization process!

Electric Fences

Once you have tried an electronic fence and created neurotic or problem behaviors, you are in for major retraining. You cannot simply go back and erase the behaviors. Please consider carefully before purchasing these inhumane devices. Many of you may say, "But my dog only had to go through the fence line once, and then he always stayed in the yard. What's the big deal?"

There *is* a big deal, but it is one you may not recognize at first as relating to the electric fence.

Learning through association takes place twenty-four hours per day, seven days per week, whether intentional or not. Add intense pain to those associations, and you have a recipe for disaster.

Your dog goes through the fence line and gets zapped by a very painful electric shock as a child, dog or car happens to pass by. He may well associate the intense pain and whatever was passing at the time. (Yes, this really happens.) From here on, you may find that your dog is terrified around that thing and, depending on his personality, will react in one of two ways: he may become either shy and fearful or extremely aggressive. A third option is also possible, that he may make no bad associations—but why take the risk?

You have an electric fence and you don't see any outward sign that there is a problem. However, a cat wanders into your yard and while your dog "respects" the electric shock fence and stays in the yard, you come home to find a dead cat (redirected aggression from the electric shock fence.)

Your dog may start to become neurotic about weird things or become timid, fearful or aggressive. He may start to become aggressive toward the other dogs you have. He may now be fearful about leaving the property at all—even in "safe" areas. He may also become fearful of new places—

especially if you use one of the "dummy" collars and leave it on all of the time. Think about it: He has a real or dummy collar on and you take him to a new location—maybe even a training class. He is now freaked out because he doesn't know where the boundaries are and is terrified of being shocked. He moves around slowly and cautiously since he doesn't know where the "safe" places are.

Okay, let's now look at the logistical problems with electric shock fences. (Notice how I don't use the term "invisible fence?" It is too easy to forget what they actually do—*shock your dog with an electric current*—when one uses the generic terminology. I don't want you to forget what this device does.) You have an electric fence. It may keep your dog within the boundaries, but does it keep out the rotten kids who want to torment your dog, other dogs—both good ones and "bad" ones—cats, skunks, squirrels, bears, coyotes, fox or deer? Of course not. If your dog decides to chase these things and braves the electric current running through his neck, do you *really* think he'll come back and risk more electric current? I think not!

Let's say you leave your dog outside unattended, and it starts to rain. You don't know it is raining because you are involved with something else or you aren't home in the first place. These collars have been known to malfunction and then—whammo! You have either a dead dog or one with so much neck damage that you are spending thousands of dollars in vet bills. Plus, you have a completely and utterly freaked out dog whenever it rains.

Or perhaps part of the fence line is close to a room he is in and he gets zapped with an electric shock. Now he is completely distraught because there is no safe place for him. It is also possible that he may not make the association between the fence line and the shock and becomes afraid to leave the house at all.

Windows, Barriers and Teasing Animals or Humans

Why did the chicken cross the road? To get to the other side. Why does your dog aggress at windows and barriers? Because he can't get to and investigate what's on that other side, and frustrations build. A dog that fence chases is rewarded by doing so; a person or car goes by, he barks and chases, the car and person disappear. Because the chasing "worked," he will do it again.

When animals or kids tease a dog, the dog may feel confined by the fence or leash, knowing that he lacks an escape route. Like the cornered

Dogs aggressing from both sides of the fence. Photo by P. Dennison.

rat in Konrad Lorenz's book *On Aggression,* "The fighter stakes his all because he cannot escape and can expect no mercy. This most violent form of fighting behavior is motivated by fear, by the most intense flight impulses whose natural outlet is prevented by the fact that the danger is too near; so the animal, not daring to turn its back on it, fights with the proverbial courage of desperation."

I have known cases where adults allowed kids to torment their dog, and when the dog lashed out to protect himself, they labeled him "aggressive" and either punished him further or euthanized him.

Lack of Proper Exercise and Enough Safe Chances to Just Be a Dog

Most of our dogs were not bred to be couch potatoes. Herding breeds were bred to herd cattle or sheep, sporting breeds were bred to swim and retrieve, terrier breeds were bred to hunt vermin, and so on. Picture a typical, high-energy six-year-old child forced to remain in his room, quiet and calm, for long periods of time with the expectation that, once released, he would be a model citizen. The mind boggles!

Too sedentary a life can cause anxiety and stress to build and the dog may act out in inappropriate ways, such as aggression. Now I understand that sometimes it is hard to find a safe place to let your aggressive dog get enough aerobic exercise. However, it is imperative to his mental state that you do find such a place. Be creative: visit fields that no one uses, get permission to walk

It is vital to your dog's mental state that you give him a safe place where he can just be a dog. Photo by P. Dennison.

in a cemetery, pack up your dog and drive to the nearest town that has some woods and grass. Even if you live in a big city, you can set up the play session to be safe. Bring a friend along—one that your dog likes—and have him or her act as a lookout for you, letting you know ahead of time if a person or dog is coming too close. That way you can move your dog away before he has a chance to aggress.

Long lines of fifty feet or so are great for this type of dog—the line becomes your "portable fence" with which the majority of dogs can get a lot of exercise and still be safe. A leisurely jaunt around the block on a six-foot leash is not enough exercise for most dogs; for the aggressive dog, it is fraught with other types of problems. "Hunting" with your dog—that is, allowing him to do what dogs do best, sniffing, exploring and rolling in dead and smelly things—is a great way to satisfy his needs as well as tire him out. The joy of seeing the sheer ecstasy on his face when he rolls in something really disgusting is worth the price of a bath! Mental stimulation can be a workout for dogs just as it is for people. A person with a sedentary desk job, who must juggle dates, equations, and bookwork, will arrive home just as tired as an aerobics instructor at the end of the day. Training new behaviors is positively stimulating, as well as an effective way to expend energy and build up your dog's confidence.

Lack of Basic Training

For you to be able to even start to work on your dog's aggressive issues, he *must* have at least some basic training based on *positive* methods.

Foundation behaviors and training are more fully discussed in Chapters Seven and Eight. If your dog doesn't actively want to look at you and be with you, then you cannot work on the aggression. If your dog is continually pulling away from you, doesn't respond to his name and thinks "come" means to ignore you, then he will have no choice but to aggress when he sees his particular provoking stimuli because he is unaware that there are alternative behaviors he can do. Just as a dog can learn that a person approaching is a cue to sit rather than jump, your aggressive dog can learn that a person approaching is a cue to look at you.

Accidental Reinforcement of Dominant or Dog-Aggressive Behavior

Many people living in a multiple-dog household believe that you should maintain the "rank order" of the pack by feeding the more dominant dog first. Well, we are not dogs and the dogs know this. Most people do not recognize the true leader of the pack, mistakenly assigning this promotion and title to the dog that is the biggest bully. Truly dominant dogs do not bully or use violence to get their way. By catering to the bully, you are actually reinforcing him for his inappropriate behavior.

Before I knew better, I used to feed Shadow first, thinking that he was the "alpha" of my other four dogs. Shadow would grab the food out of my hand and then bully the other dogs away or attack them in an effort to get their food or treats. Once I understood that feeding Shadow first was actually reinforcing his "bully" behavior, I taught him to have a little patience and I fed him last. Shadow now calmly waits his turn. As an added bonus, the other dogs will now come close to Shadow while treats are doled out, knowing that he will not attack them. Even if they happen to drop a treat, he leaves it alone, knowing his will be coming soon.

The true canine leader is benevolent, doesn't fight and never bullies. It is quite common that a multiple-dog household does not even have a canine leader. If you think your acting-out dog is the leader and you try to emulate his behavior in controlling him, what you are really doing is acting aggressively toward him. This way of thinking is not useful in trying to maintain a positive relationship or a good training environment.

MEDICAL PROBLEMS

While I believe that most aggression starts with a fear response and becomes a learned behavior, there are a few medical problems that masquerade as aggression. Once you realize that you have an aggression problem on your hands, it is very important that your dog be thoroughly examined by your veterinarian, hopefully one well-versed in this problem. For instance, when checking for low-normal thyroid (low-normal thyroid has been conclusively linked to aggression, although the jury is still out as to whether aggression causes low thyroid or low thyroid creates aggression), many veterinarians will read the results and conclude that your dog is within normal range, when in fact, he may not be and would benefit from Soloxine.

Louisa Beal, DVM, states that there are quite a few health problems that only look like behavioral problems. These conditions can create aggression, variable personality, depression, self-mutilation, excessive licking, temperament changes, inability to settle, pacing and circling.

Diet can exacerbate underlying medical conditions or affect behavior directly. Low magnesium, chronic lead poisoning and corticosteroid (e.g., prednisone) overdose all play a role in increasing aggression, as do poor quality foods. Most of the commercial foods on the market are loaded with indigestible proteins that could possibly even exacerbate food aggression. Standard dog foods are not nutritious, and the dogs can be actually starving—even if you over-feed. No one food can possibly be 100 percent complete. Dogs are by nature scavengers and do best with a variety of whole, fresh foods. Over-vaccination and vaccinosis (allergic reactions to vaccines) can also cause behavioral changes.

As Dr. Beal further states, "My guideline is this—any adult dog with a new problem should be checked first to see if there is an underlying medical problem."

Common Medical Conditions That May Present as Behavioral Problems

infections, distemper, Lyme disease, tumors, seizures, stroke, physical traumas, pregnancy or false pregnancy, low blood sugar, hypothyroidism (low thyroid, even without classic symptoms), intestinal problems, onset of blindness or deafness

I was working with a Collie named Geordie. All of a sudden, he was refusing to jump, sit or do a sit stay. I recommended that he be checked by a vet since he had always been a willing worker in the past. It turns out he had spondylosis (a degenerative disorder that may cause loss of normal spinal structure and function) and wasn't physically capable of doing those things anymore.

Benny, a Beagle, was depressed, aggressive and highly reactive to sights, sounds, people and dogs. He was refusing to eat his food and not all that thrilled about treats or training. Within two days of being put on a raw food diet, his depression was gone and he was very willing to be trained regarding his other issues.

After being well socialized, Tommy, a Bullmastiff, suddenly began aggressing at people. His owner knew there was something wrong—Tommy also was limping sporadically. She took him to quite a few veterinarians and they could find nothing to explain the condition—they called it a mild strain. She finally went to a specialist. It turns out that Tommy had completely ruptured a ligament and, because it went undiagnosed for so long, the joint capsule was ultimately damaged as well. The only thing holding his shoulder together was his muscle mass. Once his shoulder was operated on and Tommy healed, 99 percent of his aggression simply disappeared.

Biscuit was doing okay in training for her fears; however, her progress was slow. She seemed to be walking very stiffly, and although we all thought that was normal for her, I recommended that she be checked by a vet. She was diagnosed with Lyme disease. Once on medication, Biscuit made huge leaps in training.

Ariel was developing some aggression toward her owners, especially when being handled. I taught the owners how to desensitize her to handling. I also had them test her for Lyme disease and, sure enough, she had it. With treatment and training, it took her only a few weeks to become comfortable with petting.

POINTS TO PONDER

❖ When dealing with the decision to retrain your aggressive dog, it is imperative to change your own mind-set and actions.

❖ Your reactions to your dog's aggression that were supportive, passive, punishing, or inadvertently reinforcing helped to perpetuate and escalate the aggression.

❖ Dogs are remarkably resilient and adaptable, and can easily be retrained to learn more acceptable behaviors.

❖ It is important to have your dog's health evaluated by a qualified veterinarian to rule out physical causes of his aggressive behavior.

Acceptance Leads to Change

FACING THE FACTS

The overriding element critical to success in working with your aggressive dog is your own recognition and acceptance of your dog's issues and dedication to helping him overcome them. If you have had a problem in the past dealing with your dog's issues, I applaud you now for seeking out more help. As we all know, rescue groups or shelters will refuse to take on a dog with an aggressive history—and for good cause. There are legal ramifications if a dog injures or kills someone, and in this litigious society, the only place for these unwanted and untrained dogs is death row.

The stark reality here is that if you don't take the time to help your furry friend, no one else will.

Recognizing Aggression

The early warning signs of aggression (listed and discussed in Chapter One) are not always easy for lay people to spot. Many owners do not recognize that they are headed for trouble and just go along their merry way, unwittingly putting the dog into increasingly dangerous situations. Or they may see there is a problem, but either don't know that solutions exist or are unable to find one that works for them, and so they banish the dog to a life sentence in the basement or backyard.

Stacy's story: We always knew Sasha didn't like people, but it became more apparent when Duke, our older dog, from whom she gained much of her stability, died. I never denied that she was aggressive but did not realize to what extent it truly went until she aggressed at me when I inadvertently

25

startled her while she was sleeping. We avoided taking Sasha out in public to avoid the chances of her aggressing toward approaching people. These reactions always left me feeling like I was a bad owner, and that she was a mean dog. I was mortified and always on guard. We had chosen a shepherd because we wanted a dog that was going to be protective; however, we lacked the knowledge to balance her natural tendency to be protective with the behaviors needed for her to function in the human world. We have since learned that acting aggressively is not normal for any breed.

I am also angry at the trainers we previously worked with who encouraged us to do protection training with her without regard for her unstable temperament. Additionally, I feel guilty and angry with myself that I didn't know enough to stop using those methods.

Denial

Many people are in denial that they have an aggressive dog. Yes, sometimes even experienced trainers go into denial. Since you can't fix a problem unless you know you have one, admitting your dog is aggressive is the first step to getting help. Perhaps you raised this dog from an eight-week-old puppy or you unwittingly rescued an aggressive dog that you don't now want to return, knowing that he will be euthanized. Either way, it can be hard to admit there is a problem because of the guilt and shame attached. Why might you go into denial? *Because you desperately do not want to own an aggressive dog.*

Denial is a defense mechanism that keeps you from facing reality. It takes many forms and comes from many sides of your personality and upbringing. You may simply have wanted a family dog "just like your old dog," and find it hard to accept that your Freddie's last name turns out to be Kruger. Or you may have adopted a dog for a specific reason—perhaps therapy work or competition—and it is difficult to let go of this goal when presented with reality.

Karen was in tremendous denial of her dog's aggression directed to other dogs. On one level she knew he was aggressive and was coming to me for help. However, instead of putting his show career on hold until the problem had improved, she insisted on entering him in breed conformation shows. Because her goal for him was foremost in her mind, she ignored the plain fact that he wasn't ready to be in a show situation and continued to deny that his problem was serious. The last show he was in was terrible— he was constantly growling and snapping at the other dogs and became completely freaked out from arousal overload.

It can be painful to give up a dog or a goal. It may leave you feeling like a failure. The long-term solution of extensive reconditioning and training may not be palatable to your lifestyle and pocketbook. Perhaps you have boxed yourself in with an extremely rigid agenda; you *will* make the dog fit into your picture, the square peg *will* fit into the round hole, dammit! Denial can be extremely destructive. In trying to meet your own goals, you can become selfishly blind to your dog's distress as you put him again and again into situations he is unable to handle, where he has no choice but to fail. Consistent denial will exacerbate the problem, not rectify it.

You must face it: The reality is that your particular dog may *never* be able to fulfill your dreams for him or for yourself. If you are to proceed with helping him, you must let go of your picture. You may be able, in a few years, to attain your goal, or you may never be able to achieve your dream. The good news is that, however bad the dog is, he can be trained to be a whole lot better.

Don't overlook or underestimate the "love" factor in the equation. In spite of the fact that your dog can frighten or sadden you, you still love him. Like the parent of a child who possesses some out-of-control behaviors, you find that interspersed with the anger and frustration are deep, positive emotions, not the least powerful of which is love. Anger and confusion can muddy other emotions, leaving you spinning, perplexed. Dogs that are reactive in public often are "perfect" when alone at home. You may find it hard to accept that this creature so loving with you is the same one that wants to take out the jugular of the UPS guy.

Expectations versus Reality

What are your expectations of your dog and of yourself as owner? In a perfect world you walk your dog off leash and he faithfully stays right beside you. He is always a model citizen, and greets all strangers in a friendly or calm manner. He always comes when called, no matter what distractions are present. He sits beside you, with his adoring head resting on your knee, always perfectly obedient. He is playful when it suits you, and when it doesn't, he lies down quietly. Add in the little bonuses of fetching the newspaper and your slippers, never jumping, barking or soiling the house, and understanding perfectly everything you say, all without effort or formal training on your part. In a perfect world, dogs come out of their mother's womb completely trained. What a wonderful, rosy picture!

Unfortunately, you don't live in that world—it doesn't exist—and that isn't the dog you have.

Reality is quite different. Owning an aggressive dog is very traumatic. Societal expectations, holding out an often simplistic, Norman Rockwell-type image, may lead you to feel disgraced or humiliated about your animal. You may think that it is a reflection of you as a person and as a dog owner, that people view you as an ineffectual, bad person because you can't control your dog. You may believe that you've "failed" your dog in some way and may start to view yourself in a bad light. It can be easier to deny that a problem exists and make hidden allowances for the dog than to face it head on.

Having company over or going for a walk can be very stressful with an aggressive dog around. The mere presence of guests or people walking by can send your dog into attack mode. You feel impotent and angry because you don't know what to do and you don't have the tools to help your dog. Helplessness leads to hopelessness, which may end in relinquishment or even euthanasia of the dog.

This is no way to live. Thank goodness, it doesn't have to be this way. But to change your dog, you must first take a good look at yourself.

PEER PRESSURE

Peer pressure means that you feel demands (either from inside or outside yourself) to be like other people. Although not all peer pressure is bad—it plays a big role in determining who you are and how you dress and talk and act—it can cause problems as well. It may be that when in a group you act differently and do things you'd never do on your own. Why? Because you lose at least some of your identity in a group. And the normal controls you put on your behavior can crumble because of the need you feel to fit in and be respected by others. Peer pressure does not affect only teenagers.

Peer pressure may cause you to react badly to your dog who is reacting badly. Unfortunately, the old mind-set in dog training still exists. You have to "show the dog what he did wrong," and "show him who's boss"; let's also not forget the ever-popular, "You can't let him get away with that." Owning an aggressive dog is hard enough to deal with and it is tempting to listen to negative pressure. You want to fit in, be liked and may feel uncomfortable going against traditional techniques. The thought "everyone else punishes their dog for aggressing" may influence you to leave your better judgment in the closet.

Inner strength and self-confidence can help you stand firm, walk away, and resist reacting badly to your dog just to satisfy someone else's needs.

June's positive solution to peer pressure: I have a dog-reactive dog, Jesse, that I show in breed and agility. She is enrolled in a program of desensitization and counterconditioning, and I am constantly manipulating consequences for her in order to set her up to learn to accept other dogs. At a recent breed show, I witnessed two separate incidents, one involving a handler performing an alpha roll on her dog and another with a dog being smashed across the face and then strung up for aggressing at another male dog. Since people want the satisfaction of seeing reactive dogs punished, the crowd purred their approval, "Yes, the handlers did the right things."

Meanwhile, Jesse snapped at a dog when she found herself completely boxed in by nearby dogs. I immediately drew upon three foundation behaviors (Jesse, come! Jesse, sit! Jesse, stay!), and reinforced her for the third behavior.

Everyone was livid. How dare I let my dog "get away" with that behavior? When questioned by the breeder, I told her that punishing my dog and ruining all my good work with her was out of the question.

However, I started thinking. What if I could make it look like I was punishing my dog, to satisfy the general public, while not really punishing her? I have never yelled at Jesse, so it was easy to teach her that any screamed words simply mean, "You are about to get a treat." Thus, my yelling at her is not a punishment at all: "NO BITE!" (good girl, cookies are coming); "KNOCK IT OFF!" (good girl, cookies are coming); "LEAVE IT!" (good girl, cookies are coming). As far as I know, the dogs that received the horrible corrections at that show are not being shown anymore, while, in the end, Jesse stopped aggressing completely in addition to earning her breed championship and Bull Terrier Club of America Versatility Award this year. "GOOD! No attack the other dogs, Jesse!"

Because you so want to do the right things for your dog, it is very difficult to avoid responding to negative peer pressure from authority figures such as veterinarians, judges, traditional trainers, well-meaning friends and family. It takes a *lot* of determination and understanding of the retraining process. Be sure to follow the advice you would give your teenagers, "Stay away from the kids who are bad influences."

Does your dog have an aggression problem? Take this simple quiz:

- Would you rather parachute into enemy territory with the Navy SEALS than take your dog for a walk?

- Do you only go out with your dog at midnight or 4 a.m. and wish you had an infrared camera to detect and then avoid anyone else who might be around?

- Do you stop breathing or panic when someone approaches? (Do you ever breathe at all when you are walking your canine buddy?)

- Have you rearranged your entire life to make sure that your dog doesn't see (and subsequently attack) other dogs or people?

- Are you embarrassed by the way your dog behaves when people come to your house?

- Are people nervous when they come to your house?

- Do people still actually come to your house?

- Do you worry about losing your home insurance if the insurance company finds out you have a dog that throws himself at the door in a frenzy whenever someone rings the doorbell?

- Do you get tired of coming up with clever responses to people who scream, "You should learn to control that dog!"

- Do you feel like a failure because your dog growls and/or lunges at people or dogs?

SELF-SABOTAGE

We have all done it—sabotaged our progress in life at one time or another. We may trip ourselves up in various ways while trying to achieve goals such as losing weight, quitting smoking, getting the perfect job, experiencing rewarding relationships and achieving success. Change is hard, and it is at times much easier for us to stay the same. There is immense comfort in what is already known. Fear of the unknown prevents us from taking chances and perhaps making changes for the better. Taking those steps toward a more meaningful outcome requires hard work, stamina, and unfailing commitment.

Living with aggressive dogs can sap our energy, leaving us with little reserve or energy needed to undertake even the first steps. Sometimes, of course, we fear failure, but at other times we actually fear success. Because change is so hard, we may sabotage our dogs' recovery, and although we seem to be serious about retraining our dogs, we continually put them in positions *to* aggress.

Sue worked with her aggressive dog, Lady, for many years. There were short periods of time throughout the years when

Lady almost stopped aggressing completely. Although Sue was getting a great deal of positive attention when her dog was doing well, she was unable to live with the fact that Lady might become more normal. Sue then sabotaged the training sessions so that Lady started aggressing again and with more intensity. Sue tried many different trainers, behaviorists and drugs for Lady to rectify the problem, but in reality, the problem was not Lady's. When Sue finally realized that she was afraid of success, she began to make better decisions with her dog.

Sometimes, as difficult as it is to imagine, you may realize that you are deriving secondary gains from owning an aggressive dog. The attention, praise and support received from trainers and behaviorists for your "valiant" efforts and continued dedication can be extremely reinforcing— even more reinforcing than actually fixing your dog.

REACTIONS OF YOUR DOG TO YOUR STRESS

Once your dog has shown his aggressive side, you may anticipate his response to various situations with your own fear reactions. Your tension fuels the fire of his aggression and a vicious cycle begins. You will probably react by doing one or more of the following: becoming alarmed, tensing up, jerking or yanking back on the leash, yelling, screaming, hitting, comforting or consoling the dog, holding your breath. Unfortunately, all of these things only encourage aggression in your dog because your fear and tension signal to the dog that "Yes, this person/dog/child is something threatening and must warded off with an aggressive display."

A student relates: Last night my husband Dale and I were walking and holding hands. All of a sudden he tightened his grip and pulled me closer. My immediate response was "Oh no! What's wrong?!" I had nearly walked into an ant pile. It made me realize what I am conveying to my dog when I choke up on the collar: "Oh, no! Trouble ahead!" I know you taught us this in class but it really brought the point home.

CONTROLLING YOUR OWN STRESS

For most of this book, I will be talking about retraining the canine half of your team. However, your stress reactions to your dog's behavior also have a major impact on his recovery. You may be very sensitized now to his previously provoking stimuli and may choke and panic when a person or dog approaches, even if your dog doesn't react anymore. It is just as important for you to learn to control your emotions as it is for your dog.

There are quite a few breathing and positive mental imagery exercises as well as stretching exercises that you can practice to help alleviate your own stress, thus helping your dog remain calm. These are the same ones used for performance anxiety by athletes, public speakers and people who compete in dog sports. You'll find them extremely valuable if you practice them diligently. Below are my three personal favorites. I have found them to be profoundly effective. There are book references in Appendix 2 for those of you who wish to learn more.

Belly Breathing

There are two kinds of breathing—chest breathing and belly breathing. Chest breathing is used for fight-or-flight responses and belly breathing is used for relaxation. Pay attention to your breathing while you are relaxed—are you breathing with your belly? Now concentrate on your breathing while you are stressed—are you breathing with your chest? You can even watch your dog while he is resting—he will be doing belly breathing. When out with your dog, you want to be breathing with your belly—the relaxed type of breathing.

Start this exercise lying on the floor. Put your hand on your stomach and breathe in through your nose for a count of five and concentrate on expanding your belly rather than your chest. Hold it for five seconds and slowly exhale through your nose to a count of five. Repeat at least ten times per session and try to do at least five sessions per day for a few weeks. Once you are comfortable doing this lying down, try it while sitting, then standing and then walking.

Positive Mental Imagery

Once you are relaxed, continue to do belly breathing and visualize yourself walking down the street or trail with your dog. For the first step, just breathe and feel yourself enjoy the walk. There are no dogs and no people—just you and your dog and nature. Practice this as many times as it takes for you to remain calm.

For the second step, visualize walking with your dog and seeing one person or dog in the far distance. Picture each and every detail of that walk—the feel of the ground under your feet; the feel of the leash in your hand; the sound of your relaxed breath; your dog heeling attentively, being calm, sitting when you stop, moving with you when you move and calmly and coolly passing that person or dog. Be sure to continue to do belly breathing while doing this exercise. Practice this as many times as it takes for you to be calm for the entire process.

Rehearse these exercises a few times per day for a few weeks in the lying down, sitting and walking positions. Gradually (just as you will add complexities when training your dog) make the visualizations a little harder—for example, you may picture two people with or without dogs in front of you and a bicycle coming up behind.

Once you become comfortable with your visualizations, bring your dog out and practice while actually walking him. While you are alone with him, don't forget to do your belly breathing and pretend, *really* pretend, that you see someone coming in the distance to activate your positive mental imagery and belly breathing. You can even make a person approaching a *cue* for you to do belly breathing. Repeat the exercises enough and you will be amazed at the results. When something does come down the pike, you will go automatically into your breathing and imagery scenes and get safely past the scary bad things.

You cannot practice these exercises once in a while and expect them to work. You need to do them quite often so that they become second nature.

Your Safe Place

There are times when we all need a little help. Your safe place can be picturing an actual safe haven—your bedroom, the beach, a protective bubble—or it can be imagining that a person who you take great comfort from (and who your dog loves) is right next to you and will protect you and your dog from harm.

> You must systematically desensitize yourself as well as your dog to the scary bad things.

Find a relaxed position, run through your breathing and imagery exercises and then imagine yourself in your safe place. Practice this so much that you think, "Scotty has just beamed me up." Now add this to your breathing and imagery repertoire while you take your dog out for a walk. Every time you see your dog's scary thing, you will instantly be beamed up into your safe place where you can breathe (hyperventilating doesn't count as breathing—I checked) and walk calmly and confidently past the object without incident or reaction from your dog.

Don't doubt the power of these exercises. Much research has been done by sports psychologists in the past several decades on the healing power of mental imagery. Athletes who have experienced injuries and are preparing to return to the "field," although physically healed, often suffer fears and anxieties that prevent them from performing at a pre-injury level. If you're still skeptical, think of how your body reacts after awakening from a nightmare. Your heart may be racing, you're likely soaked in perspiration and breathing rapidly. These physical symptoms are the result of mental imagery.

Through controlled mental imagery, you have the ability to manipulate the course of events. Set the scene, add the characters, and control the outcome. Positive mental imagery has been proven to build confidence and alleviate fears. In order to fully utilize the powers of mental imagery, you need to be in a relaxed state. This is why belly breathing and finding your safe place are even more valuable. The combination of these three relaxation techniques will most assuredly assist you in situations where you may have previously panicked.

Just as you must systematically desensitize your dog using foundation behaviors, you need to give yourself alternative behaviors. Otherwise you will limit yourself and your dog. I've learned firsthand how well these exercises work. Were it not for them, I would not be able to compete successfully in agility and Rally with my dog Shadow—or even go for a walk on the trail or street.

I had entered my aggressive Border Collie, Shadow, in his first APDT Rally trial. I knew I would have to work on belly breathing, positive mental imagery and being in my safe place. In addition, knowing this was an indoor show site, I practiced door etiquette. I had people stand in the doorway and come in and go out as Shadow and I went in and out. I then added other dogs and tried to practice as much as possible taking him calmly into a busy building.

I was calm, cool, and collected during my drive to the show site. I got there an hour early and took Shadow out of the van. He was completely and utterly inattentive. I panicked and started hyperventilating. I put him back in the van. After about a half-hour, I brought him out again—I wanted to practice going in and out of the building. He could not focus on me, and I became completely freaked out, angry and disappointed. I put him back in the van, slammed the door and started screaming as I walked around the parking lot. I was sorely disappointed that, after all of the work we had done, he couldn't focus on me.

Although I found that I wasn't able to control my breathing, I was finally able to practice positive mental imagery and being in my safe place. These exercises helped, and Shadow and I both relaxed.

After we had our run, I went back in and saw that Shadow had gotten a score of 198 out of a possible 200 and won the class!

There was another trial later that day, and Shadow and I were both composed and confident. He was wonderful again! He got a third place with a score of 197! I still was unable to do the belly breathing, so I just concentrated on being in my safe place and positive mental imagery.

The moral here was that I was lucid enough to be able to switch gears when Shadow was incapable of doing one behavior (proper door etiquette); I didn't let it affect our entire day—and our subsequent wins and placements.

KEEP YOUR EYE ON THE GOAL

As you read through these pages, you will see the importance of making clear, realistic and concise goals for your dog at any given time. If your goal is to compete in, say, agility, and your dog is reactive to other dogs from 100 yards away, then it would be wise to put that goal on the back burner for now. If your goal is to be able to walk on the trail and your dog is lunging at every passerby, you too, need to revise this end goal.

Your initial aspiration simply might be to have your dog live through one full day without any type of reaction. That one day will build to two days, then three days and so on. If you slowly and carefully set up your training regimen, there will come a time when you won't even remember how "bad" your dog once (past tense!) was.

When you have reached that stage, many new frontiers will be waiting for you. For instance, if you are looking at competition as a future possibility, APDT Rally obedience has no stand for exam in level one and no group stays in any level. Agility requires no direct contact from either people or dogs.

If you are looking at "just" having a great companion, I can think of no greater goal than the AKC Canine Good Citizen test. This is a milestone and real achievement to mark the retraining of your dog.

POINTS TO PONDER

❧ *Your mind-set is a major component of your success in retraining your dog.*

❧ *You must see your dog as he is, not as you wish him to be, and go on from there.*

❧ *Controlling your own stress level is an important factor in controlling your dog's stress.*

Prevention Is the Best Cure

TRAINING TO PREVENT AGGRESSION

The socialization process should start as soon as you get your pup and continue for at least eight to eighteen months. Even if you socialize your dog as a young pup, you must persist with the program through adolescence. The list of who and what your dog will accept needs to remain open. If you stop at any time before twelve to eighteen months, you run the risk of the dog "forgetting" that he has been exposed to certain things. As the dog moves through adolescence, his instinct to mistrust "outsiders" increases and continuing socialization is needed.

There are numerous viewpoints on how old a puppy should be to start training/socializing. There is a small window of opportunity here—between eight and twenty weeks—when the puppy is most able to benefit from early socialization and training. In reality, a great deal of exposure must be started even earlier, when the pup is still with Mom and littermates. There is a concern about starting training classes before the puppy's immunizations have been completed, but that attitude is changing. In my opinion, the benefits of early training and socialization far outweigh the risk of disease. The bottom line for me is that there is more risk of euthanasia due to behavioral problems than there is risk from diseases.

I like to start training pups at the age of nine weeks. They have already had their first puppy shots, plus they still retain some immunity from their mom. It is also a big benefit that their owners haven't yet had the chance to react inappropriately to the typical annoying puppy behaviors. These young pups soak up knowledge like little furry sponges. The training doesn't have to be rigorous—simple things like making eye contact, recognizing their names, following Mom around, learning the bathroom is outside, playing with new toys, sniffing new objects, meeting new friendly people and playing with other puppies, plus learning sit and down are fine for younger puppies. If you use positive training, you can start training even earlier, teaching the puppy to love learning. I have known some people who start clicker training an entire litter of puppies at four to six weeks of age.

Jane is teaching a five-week-old puppy to balance on a board with a tennis ball under it. Photo by P. Dennison.

DEBUNKING THE ALPHA DOG MODEL

The fundamental science of dog training applies to every dog of every breed. A dog is a dog is a dog. Having said that, yes, there are different breed characteristics—dogs were all bred for different skills. Mostly likely, a Bull Terrier would have no clue about herding sheep and a German Shepherd Dog would probably not be interested in killing vermin. But again, a dog is a dog. The "*my* breed needs special training—a good old fashioned alpha roll will show him who's boss" road is nothing more than a shortcut to the shelter or the euthanasia room at your vet's.

Aggression fosters aggression; try to dominate *any* breed and you are asking for trouble. Will some of these dogs tolerate more punishment than others? Maybe, maybe not, but every time you use punishment on a dog, you are rolling the dice—will he become aggressive? You never know. I cannot predict with 100 percent accuracy what the result of punishment will be, but I can always predict the result of positive reinforcement with perfect accuracy. I like those odds.

Patty had been told to use a firm hand and "aggressively" socialize her eight-week-old Rottweiler pup, Robbie, meaning that she was to drag him indiscriminately to many different places and, regardless of his state of mind, force him to interact with everyone and everything. When he was at the vet's office getting his first round of puppy shots, the vet scruff-shaked him and did an alpha roll when Robbie exhibited signs of fear.

By the time Robbie was fourteen weeks old, he was a nervous wreck and aggressively fearful of every stranger he met. Patty was skeptical that positive training would work for her "tough" breed of dog, but was willing to try. Within a few sessions, Robbie was back to being the friendly pup he used to be.

Back when I was training my dogs using punishment, my Sheltie Noel would bark incessantly. Once, to shut her up, I alpha rolled her and screamed at her. She bit me. I deserved it, and I certainly never did *that* again. Did that make her a "dominant" dog, one that I had to show who was boss? Nope. She was just sitting there, minding her own business, barking her fool head off at nothing (as Shelties do sometimes) and *I* aggressed at *her*. I put her in a position where she felt she had to protect herself.

The original alpha/dominance wolf pack model resulted from short-term wolf studies conducted in the 1940s. Because the studies were only short-term and focused on the easiest aspects of wolf behavior to observe, such as hunting, more subtle interactions were not tracked. The conclusions drawn were based on less than two percent of wolf interactions. Although later and more extensive research has disproved many of the findings, this faulty model continues to be stuck in the minds of many dog trainers like gum on their shoes.

Poodles, Schnauzers, Great Danes, Border Collies, Shih Tzus, all breeds of dog on the planet are defined biologically as
Kingdom: Animalia
Phylum: Chordata
Class: Mammalia
Order: Carnivora
Family: Canidae
Genus: Canis
Species: familiaris

There is still a great deal of debate about the dominance role model—whether the model itself is fact or fiction and whether we as humans can act as true alphas with our dogs. I look at it this way: We are not dogs; dogs are not human—we cannot be true alpha dogs because we are *not* dogs. Worrying about the alpha/dominance model muddies up the waters and really does nothing to solve aggression problems. When discussing alpha rolls in her article "The History and Misconceptions of Dominance Theory," Melissa Alexander says:

> The early researchers saw this behavior and concluded that the higher-ranking wolf was forcibly rolling the subordinate to exert his dominance. Well, not exactly. This is actually an "appeasement ritual" instigated by the SUBORDINATE wolf. The subordinate offers his muzzle, and when the higher-ranking wolf "pins" it, the lower-ranking wolf voluntarily rolls and presents his belly. There is NO force. It is all entirely voluntary. A wolf would flip another wolf against his will ONLY if he were planning to kill it. Can you imagine what a forced alpha roll does to the psyche of our dogs?
>
> *(emphasis in original)*

Contrary to popular opinion, dogs that push you out of the way while going through a doorway, that bark incessantly to get what they want (possibly bullying you to "feed me my dinner *now!*"), that comply with your requests only when they feel like it, and that won't get off furniture, won't get into their crate, etc., are *not* alpha dogs. They have simply been trained by you that these things work. Experience has taught them that they can get what they want without doing what *you* want. They are bullies, pure and simple. How did they become bullies? If you, as the trainer, reward pushy, you get pushy.

Your goal is to be a benevolent leader, not an imitation of a snarling wolf.

You are in control of and responsible for providing all resources for your dog: food, water, toys (things to chew or chase), access to sleeping areas, access to outside, play, training, etc. It is your job to provide these items or your dog will go looking for them on his own. As long as you hold the keys to these resources, you have all the power and "dominance" you will ever need.

CONTINUING HIS EDUCATION

A few minutes per day of training, plus an hour or so of "school" and puppy play are an ideal start in teaching your pup that new places, dogs and people are "good," but you do need to follow up on this good beginning. In the early weeks, most puppies will meet and accept new people and dogs with ease. However, there comes a time that this changes. The people and dogs that the puppy knows are now considered his "family" and therefore "safe," while anyone met after this time becomes an "intruder," to be repelled by aggressive force if necessary. For this reason, even if you have other dogs, you must work to counteract the "us" versus "them" mentality. You must continue to take your dog to class!

Mary came to me with her two-year-old Great Dane that was showing aggressive tendencies. When obtaining the dog's history, it turns out she had never taken him off her property except for vet visits (which were pretty negative experiences). He had never been exposed to strangers, other dogs, and other sights and sounds. Naturally, he was developing a fear and mistrust of these things.

Now, there may be some dogs that, even with plenty of the right kind of socialization and contact, will still make their two lists of friends and foes. While not an ideal scenario, it is a normal one—you don't have a "lemon." We humans don't like everyone we meet and it may be a bit unrealistic to think that your dog *must* love every person or dog he meets. It is really more important in the long run that your dog accepts, tolerates and is calm around people and other dogs. Socialization is still necessary to maintain this basic tolerance of other dogs and people.

Socialize Appropriately

Sometime around five months old, a dramatic change happens with puppies. Virtually any young puppy in the world can walk up to almost any dog and do just about any obnoxious thing and the big dog (as long as he was properly socialized) will just placidly put up with it. However, at the five-month mark, the "puppy license" expires and older dogs will start to expect better behavior from the puppy. The big dogs will no longer put up with rough play or constant pestering from the youngster. It's sort of like a doggie bar mitzvah—one day they are just puppies, and the next the big dogs will look at them and say, "Today, you are a dog." At just around this time, puppies will also start seriously sorting the world out into "us" and "them." They will be deciding who is their family and who is an outsider, and it is instinctive for dogs to be less trustful of outsiders. This is why it is so critical both to get your puppy out and socialized at a young age and to continue his socialization into adolescence, when he is still amenable to accepting new people and experiences—you want your dog's "us" list to be very, very long!

Socialize Your Pup at His Own Pace

It is imperative that while you get your pup used to dogs and people, you do it at *his* pace, not your own. If at first he feels more comfortable hiding in a corner, let him be—he will come out of his shell on his own time schedule. If you force the dog to interact when he is scared, you risk creating total panic. Any shy child will tell you this.

Sally brought her Shetland Sheepdog puppy to puppy kindergarten. Marvin was quite afraid of the other dogs and hid under the desk for five weeks. Sally's friends urged her to pressure the puppy to play, but she knew

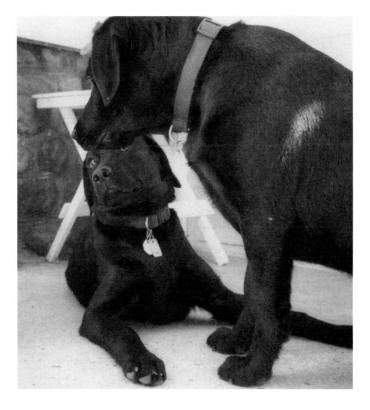

The older dog on the right is using subtle intimidation to get his point across by starting to stand over the younger dog. The younger dog is starting to move his head away and shrinking ever so slightly off to one side in acquiescence. After this shot, the older dog walked away. Photo by M. Irizarry.

better than to push. If another puppy approached him, he would scream as if his nose were stuck in a light socket. We all ignored it and by week six, Marvin came out on his own accord and became the ringleader for playtime.

Attend a Formal Class

Remember, every puppy needs socialization and interaction with new people and dogs. Even if you are the greatest dog trainer in the universe, you can't provide this for your puppy in your backyard. There is always something new to learn, so even if you have trained many other dogs, get out to a positive training class. This dog is not your other dog—each one is unique. Even littermates are not clones of each other, just as human siblings are not identical. And the issue here is not what you already know; it is what your puppy does not yet know.

PRIMARY CARETAKING: AN ADULT RESPONSIBILITY

Many people want a dog that can grow up with the kids. What they fail to realize is that owning a puppy should be a lifelong commitment to the dog. Training takes a lot of time and dedication (one puppy kindergarten is not enough training) and if soccer, football,

THE RULE OF SEVENS

By the time a puppy is seven weeks old, he should have

1. Been on seven different surfaces: carpet, concrete, wood, vinyl, grass, dirt, gravel, woodchips, etc.

2. Played with seven different types of objects: big balls, small balls, soft fabric toys, fuzzy toys, squeaky toys, paper or cardboard items, metal items, wooden items, milk jugs, etc.

3. Been in seven different locations: front yard, backyard, basement, kitchen, car, garage, laundry room, bathroom, crate, kennel, etc.

4. Met and played with seven new people, including children, older adults, and plenty of men, with and without beards.

5. Been exposed to seven challenges: climb on a box, climb off a box, go through a tunnel, climb steps, go down steps, climb over obstacles, play hide and seek, go in and out a doorway with a step up or down, run around a fence.

6. Eaten from seven different containers: metal, plastic, cardboard, paper, china, pie plate, frying pan, etc.

7. Eaten in seven different locations: crate, yard, kitchen, basement, laundry room, bathroom, x-pen, etc.

—Author Unknown

karate, cheerleading, dance, and other after-school activities take up much of your life, then do not get a dog.

Owning a puppy is a huge responsibility. If you miss the early opportunities to properly train and socialize him, you may just have a bigger problem on your hands than you bargained for. If your aggressive dog was a rescue, it is likely that socialization issues were not addressed in the first place, which is why he ended up in rescue.

DEALING WITH FEAR PERIODS

There are many fear periods that puppies go through in the early stages of their lives. Frequently, the "weird" behaviors exhibited during these times are overlooked or misunderstood. If you handle these situations incorrectly, you may end up with serious aggression problems. To me, a fear period is like having a lowered immune system—you must be extra careful about what you expose your puppy to during these times. In fact, during a fear period it is best to keep your puppy in familiar settings and *not* introduce him to new things.

Since every puppy develops at a different rate, I can't give you an exact schedule of your puppy's fear periods to put on your calendar so you know when to expect the next one. However, on average, fear periods occur within these time frames:

- Between seven to nine weeks (many reputable breeders won't send their puppies to a new home during this time because the stress of the new environment would only exacerbate this first and critical fear period)
- Around four to six months
- At approximately nine months
- At approximately twelve months
- Around fourteen to eighteen months

How do you recognize a fear period? Usually the clue is that the puppy becomes suddenly afraid of something or someone that he either ignored or liked before. The fear can manifest itself as shyness, backing away, hunching down, crouching, shaking, hiding under furniture, running away, or submissively urinating, or it may be expressed in more active "go away!" behaviors, such as growling, raising of hackles, barking or baring teeth while backing up and/or making himself small.

While your puppy is in one of the fear periods, it is important that you not take him to any new places or introduce him to new people, and most certainly, unless absolutely necessary, don't take him to the vet. If you are going to a puppy k class, as long as it is familiar to the puppy, you can keep going. His mental state is vulnerable at these times, so he may react vehemently to something he normally wouldn't blink an eye at. You won't have to totally isolate him during these times, just keep away from anything new or potentially scary.

If punishment is doled out to the puppy when he is afraid and showing signs of aggression, the stage may be set for future problems. It is important to understand that these puppies are *afraid* and are trying to protect themselves from what they perceive as life threatening. It doesn't matter that you know for a fact that the drainpipe or Uncle Todd will not harm the puppy—the *puppy* doesn't know that. You must create pleasant associations with the scary thing—that is the only way to convince the puppy that his fears are unfounded.

Tom's young Cocker Spaniel, Suzie, all of a sudden developed a fear of people coming to the house. While she was barking, growling and snarling, Tom alternately cajoled and chastised her, in an attempt to show her that there was nothing to be afraid of. Eventually, Suzie became so fearful of strangers that when guests came to the house, she had to be either put into a separate room or boarded at a friend's house.

Tom understandably thought that by comforting his dog, he was assuring her that everything was all right and she would stop being afraid of the visitors. He was also embarrassed by her behavior, which manifested itself in yelling at her. Unfortunately, he was actually reinforcing the "bad" behavior and Suzie just became more and more aggressive toward strangers. What could he have done differently? He could have ignored Suzie's fearful behaviors and *once she calmed down on her own,* paired food, petting and praise with new people. That would have created a pleasant association between visitors

Any time your dog becomes afraid, make a mental note of when and how it happened so you can avoid or be prepared for that situation in the future.

and food, and in no time Suzie would have been eagerly anticipating new people.

Your best bet is to slowly and carefully set up the situation so that the dog isn't afraid in the first place. If, despite your best management, your puppy becomes afraid, be silent and wait for him to feel more comfortable, and then reward him for calm, confident behavior. You can reinforce for "bravery." If the pup is afraid of an object, you can reinforce him for sniffing, approaching or going under or on top of that object. You must be careful, however; you don't want to be a "cheerleader." If you cheer while the dog is afraid, you are reinforcing the fearful behavior, so be sure to *cheer while the dog is doing the "brave" behavior.*

I had a puppy in puppy kindergarten that was afraid of the hanging plants in the window. She was so frightened she couldn't focus, and kept watching the scary bad plants out of the corner of her eye. I took down the plants and placed them on the floor with a trail of food leading up to and into the plants. We said nothing to her and just stood there quietly while she was afraid. As she started to move toward the plants, we softly cheered her on. Sure enough, within two minutes, she had her nose buried in the plants, snuffling for more. She worked the entire rest of the class next to the now "good" plants, with her tail gently wagging, occasionally checking to be sure she hadn't missed a treat.

BASIC LESSONS EVERY PUPPY MUST LEARN

Accepting Handling

Your dog will need to be handled throughout his life by many people—veterinarians, groomers, friends, family and boarding kennel workers. It is imperative to his own peace of mind that you teach your pup to willingly and calmly accept handling from the earliest possible moment. Toenail clipping should not be a battle of wills, with four burly vet techs having to hold the dog down.

One of my students asked me to help clip her dog's nails. I fed the dog while she clipped. Because of the desensitization work we had done with handling, it took all of about ninety seconds to complete the clipping. When we were done, my student had a look of incredulity on her face. I asked her what was wrong. She said, "It used to take me sixteen days to clip her nails—one nail per day!"

If your young dog bites you when you try to handle him (during brushing, petting, etc.), then you need to teach him that examining him is a good thing and something to be enjoyed.

Jacky brought her nine-week-old Lab puppy Roscoe to me for training. He was extremely touch-sensitive and wouldn't let Jacky or anyone else touch him without biting—and biting hard. I saw the potential for disaster and put Jacky and Roscoe on a "let me touch you for all of your daily needs" regimen. Touch—get a treat; touch—get to go outside; touch—get a toy to play with; touch—get a drink; touch—get a meal. Within a few weeks, Roscoe was welcoming petting and now, almost three years later, is continuing to enjoy physical contact.

Not all dogs enjoy petting. If you have one that doesn't, don't try to force yourself on him, thinking that will solve the problem. He can learn to enjoy it, however, if you pair good things with your handling.

Owner feeding while handling a puppy.
Photo by P. Dennison.

Sensible House Training

Using the outside bathroom is a human issue, not a dog issue. Using the toilet instead of a diaper is a parent issue, not a baby issue. Just as you wouldn't punish your child for messing his diaper, don't punish your dog for messing the house. Punishing him for eliminating in the house will create fear of you or fear of eliminating anywhere near you. It is an easy thing to simply reinforce the puppy for going outside and then manage his life so that he is unlikely to make mistakes. Take him out frequently, after meals, play, and naps, and don't let him run all over the house (he *will* piddle) until he has developed enough physiologically to hold it in.

Appropriate Use of Mouth

Puppies bite and chew. (Incidentally, it is only by biting that they learn to inhibit their bite.) It is how they relate to their world, much in the same way a toddler puts everything in his mouth, although some puppies may be more mouthy than others. The pain of teething also certainly has a lot to do with this behavior. It is how you react to this inevitable biting that can create the problem. If you pay excessive attention to the mouthing, then you are reinforcing it. Set your pup up right in the first place—give him chew toys or pay attention to him *before* he bites, or simply, quietly and instantly leave the room if he makes contact with your body. Many times, the puppy is simply overtired and needs a nap, so just put him in his crate when you see the early signs of "crankiness."

You must be careful not to play too roughly with your pup. He can become overaroused and, not knowing how to stop you (after all, he doesn't speak English), may lash out and bite. It is simply not fair to whip him up into a frenzy and then expect him to have self-control and stop instantly. If things do get out of hand, simply tuck him away in his crate or pen for a rest, without any comment or scolding.

Sharing

You have to train the dog to share—his natural inclination is to hoard. He will not be willing to "give" unless you have taught this behavior properly. If you simply wrest toys from him or take away his food without offering a nice exchange first, your dog is going to start guarding things from you.

Look at it this way: Suppose I follow you to work on payday and force you to give me your paycheck. Next week, I do the same thing. By the third week, you'll be coming to work with a gun to make sure I don't get your paycheck again. Well, dogs can't use a gun, but they have those effective teeth.

Candy was told by her breeder to never allow her Giant Schnauzer puppy, Stanley, to pick up or chew a pinecone. In response to those instructions, Candy would wrest anything and everything out of his mouth. This set the stage for a lifelong guarding problem of food, toys, anything Stanley felt was his.

PROTECTING YOUR DOG

Always monitor your dog's interactions with other dogs and people. Well-meaning people may force themselves on a puppy in an unintentionally inappropriate and aggressive manner. That can frighten your puppy. If the puppy jumps, many people will use the old "traditional" response of kneeing him in the chest or yanking down on the collar, creating an association between strangers and pain. Young children can be too rough, not understanding that their behavior (yanking, pulling, poking, hitting, kicking) actually hurts. You must be vigilant at all times and protect your puppy from inappropriate contact with people.

You can always make it a simple management issue: If you have guests over that you sense or know are not dog-friendly, won't be gentle with your puppy or won't listen to your directions, then by all means keep your puppy away from these people. You wouldn't allow friends or strangers hurt or traumatize your child, so please don't let them do this to your puppy.

Socialize with Appropriate Dogs

It is imperative to let your puppy play only with friendly dogs. Most puppy kindergartens have puppies of around the same age and size. You can always form your own play group with other students, friends and neighbors, to keep the socialization going.

In one of my puppy kindergarten classes, there was a puppy that was too rough and too aroused to be able to play within the group. She was scaring the other puppies, so I pulled her out of playtime and put her behind

Arjay had been grooming Nelson (the dog lying down flat on the ground) when the puppy came over. Arjay didn't want to be bothered and gave a slight warning—lip just starting to rise, brow just starting to furrow and ears off to the sides. Photo by M. Irizarry.

The puppy is not backing off Arjay's subtler signals and so he has to use more obvious ones—lips high enough now to show teeth (but face is not pushed forward), and brow furrowed even more. After this photo the older dog eased up on the puppy as the puppy backed off. Photo by M. Irizarry.

some baby gates. We fed her for calm behaviors while she watched the other puppies. At the end of class, I brought in one of my adult dogs to interact with her—one that I knew would not hurt her in any way and would play with her only if she was calm. After a few sessions, she was able to rejoin the play group.

It is also important to keep the play sessions short. Even the best of "pals" can get overtired and overaroused and end up squabbling. Depending on the severity of the tiff, how often you let it happen, and the innate personality of the dog himself, this can end up creating dog aggression. As with protecting your dog against overbearing and possibly punishing people, you must protect your dog from tyrannical or aggressive dogs.

POINTS TO PONDER

❧ *Get rid of the old dominance role model—whether or not it is valid really doesn't matter. Work with the behaviors you need, rather than getting stuck in a debate that ultimately is pointless.*

❧ *You must watch your dog carefully for early warning signs of aggression or fear, and teach him to accept what he is afraid of.*

❧ *Reinforce your dog for being brave, and be careful you don't cheerlead while he is afraid.*

❧ *A few weeks of training is not enough to yield you a well-trained dog. After all, we humans go to school for a minimum of twelve years—and we, supposedly, are the smarter species.*

❧ *No matter the breed, all dogs respond better to positive reinforcement.*

❧ *If your puppy is to be well socialized, he must be exposed to many friendly people and dogs until he is at least eighteen months old.*

Understanding How Your Dog Learns

To better understand your dog, how he relates to our human world and how to mend his aggression problem, you will need to understand how classical conditioning and operant conditioning work. These are the tools you will use to rehabilitate your dog. I will try not to confuse you with too much science—that isn't what this book is about. There are excellent resources at the back of the book for those of you that want to read further.

CLASSICAL CONDITIONING

Classical conditioning takes place when something that has no particular meaning for the dog *(a neutral stimulus)*, such as a tone or light, becomes associated with something that does have meaning for the dog, such as food or water, physical pain or pleasure.

This pairing can cause reflexive behaviors to occur—most commonly known would be salivating or blinking and emotions. This new reflex is said to be conditional, in that the response depends upon the stimulus having been associated with a previously existing reflex.

So what does that mean in plain English and how does it relate to your dog? Well, for example, a can opener has no meaning for a new puppy. Then you open up a can of dog food and feed him. After you do this a few times, the puppy will associate the can opener with being fed. Like Pavlov's dog, your puppy may actually begin to drool at the sight of the can opener. Drooling is an inborn natural reflexive action that can now be produced by the appearance of a can opener—a hunk of metal that originally had no particular meaning for the puppy.

You pick up a piece of leather, attach it to your dog's collar and take him for a walk in the park. At first, the leash has no meaning for the dog. However, it will quickly take on the meaning that something fun is going to happen, and pretty soon the sight of the leash will cause your dog to become very excited. Emotions can also be considered a natural reflex. A rolled-up newspaper can be a harmless object unless you hit your dog with it. Then the sight of a rolled-up newspaper can elicit fear from the dog. The fear response, perhaps in the form of avoidance or submissive postures, is the behavior you now see. Both of these emotions—excitement and fear—can be evoked through classical conditioning, and previously neutral objects can now elicit emotional responses.

A neutral stimulus can be anything—a sofa, a drainpipe, a stranger, a car—that originally has no value whatsoever for the dog in either a threatening or a nonthreatening sense. "Becomes associated with" indicates the experience you pair with that initially meaningless item. The most important lesson you need to learn is that, if good things are always happening around you, strange dogs, new people and all sorts of things, you will have a well-adjusted pet that you can take anywhere. If bad things are always happening around these stimuli, your dog will *learn* to be fearful toward them.

If, when confronted by an unfamiliar object or situation, your dog shows an anxiety response such as growling or baring his teeth in an attempt to protect himself, and you pair an aversive (punishment) with the object in an attempt to stop your dog's reactions, *he will learn to be even more fearful* and may possibly turn that fear into a more aggressive response to keep the scary thing away.

Dogs are generally aggressive because they have had a bad experience with a particular stimulus. That stimulus might be a person, dog, object or a certain place (the vet's office, for instance). It is important to know what stimuli "trigger" bad associations for your dog. If your dog has had a bad experience with a particular stimulus,

> Whenever I rescue a new dog, I always change his name and his "come" word. I don't know what kind of bad associations he may have had in the past with these important words, so we start out fresh with only positive associations.

you will need to change that association and make sure that all future encounters with the dog's provoking stimulus are pleasant ones (this is *counterconditioning*). Pairing good things with scary things helps to dissipate the fear. I will be talking more about the counterconditioning process later on.

OPERANT CONDITIONING

Classical conditioning is largely responsible for your *reflexive*—that is, your automatic, involuntary—response in any situation. For example, you smell bread baking, and you feel hungry and possibly even start salivating. Operant behavior is *voluntary* behavior that is influenced by its consequences. You smell bread baking and get out a plate and some butter, and you get to eat fresh bread as a consequence. Whether wanted behaviors occur in the future depends upon the nature of the consequence. If doing the behavior makes life better for you (or your dog), it will most likely happen again in the future.

By itself classical conditioning isn't of much value, except that it provides the motivation or emotions to act; the action is the "operant" part of the behavior. You want your dog to learn behaviors that you find useful. How do you start to teach him? It is as easy as remembering your ABCs. There are three "ingredients" for teaching any trained behavior—Antecedent (or cue), Behavior and Consequence. You say "sit" (antecedent), the dog sits (behavior), and you reward the dog with a treat (consequence of that behavior). Your dog's sitting behavior will increase because it was rewarded in a positive way. Or, say, a person approaches your human-aggressive dog (antecedent), your dog aggresses (behavior), and the person goes away or you drag the dog away (consequence). Your dog's aggressive behavior will increase because his behavior was rewarded—he was able to get away from the scary thing.

Why is this important to know? I want you to know how to break inappropriate behaviors down into cue (antecedent), behavior and consequence so that if you run into a problem, you'll know how to fix it. If you change the consequence for the dog, you can modify the behavior. Depending on the situation, you may also revise the meaning of the cue, and so also change the behavior. Counterconditioning is as simple as this.

Altering your dog's view of the cue is called *desensitization*. In this process it is vital that you don't put your dog in a position where he can fail. To break the chain, you need to teach your dog that when he sees his

To change problem behaviors, you can

Change the consequence: You can teach your dog that calm, quiet behaviors gets him what he wants, rather than pushy, obnoxious behaviors;

or

Change the meaning of the cue: You can teach your dog that the cue of the doorbell ringing now means to run to his crate, rather than to charge the door.

particular trigger, great things happen to him. He will begin to make new associations with the old trigger and eventually will change his behavior and its consequences.

Desensitization is a procedure in which the dog is exposed to extremely low levels (distance, duration) of a frightening stimulus while wonderful things (the best food, toys, play, petting, praise) are happening to him (while he is calm). The level of the frightening stimulus is gradually increased, but never at a rate that causes him distress.

Antecedents, or **cues**, are simply anything that comes *before* a behavior. The can opener, the little clicking sound that a computer makes as it shuts off, or a hand signal or verbal cue can all be antecedents, or cues.

Behaviors are the actions that are motivated by the cue. The can of food being opened causes your dog to get excited and run around the house and bark, the clicking off of your computer induces your dog to jump up from a sound sleep and race to the bed in preparation for night-night time, and the hand signal or verbal cue tells your dog to sit.

Consequences are what happen to the dog or person as a direct result of performing the behavior. Your dog gets to eat, you and your dog cuddle on the bed, and your dog gets a treat for sitting.

There are basically two kinds of consequences of behavior—those that you like and those you don't. The above examples are all positive consequences based on the behaviors presented. Your actions (and your dog's actions) can lead to something either added (*positive*) to the environment or taken away (*negative*). The terms *positive* and *negative* do not infer value or moral judgments on whether the *behavior* is good or bad—simply whether or not a consequence is being *added* to the environment (*positive*), or being *taken away* from the environment (*negative*). Additionally, punishment means that a behavior *decreases* and reinforcement means that a behavior *increases*.

Learning and behavior is really much more complex than this, but this is a good starting point for understanding operant behavior.

The definition of learning is "a change in behavior due to experience." Most certainly, as positive trainers, we want those experiences to be pleasant ones and the behaviors of our dogs to be calm and accepting. We all know that behavior is influenced by its consequences. We reward or punish people and dogs so that they will behave in different ways.

Positive Reinforcement

Your dog offers a behavior that pleases you and you give him a treat; his "good" behavior will increase. You have added something to the environment (positive) that increases (reinforces) the behavior. Be it keeping "four on the floor," going potty outside, walking on a loose leash, or looking calmly at a provoking stimulus; if a behavior is positively reinforced, it will increase. Using positive reinforcement is the most humane way of training. Positive reinforcement helps to make it clearer to your dog exactly what you are looking for. The dog learns faster and retains that learning longer. You are able to practice to practice gentleness and real teaching, rather than reacting with anger to

THE MENU OF CONSEQUENCES OF BEHAVIOR

Positive reinforcement, positive punishment, negative reinforcement and negative punishment are the main terms of consequences, and these can be very confusing at first. Remember that the terms "positive" and "negative" relate only to adding something or taking something away, and the terms "reinforcement" and "punishment" relate only to whether behavior increases or it decreases.

Positive Reinforcement (+R) — Anything added (positive) *(that your dog likes)* that *increases* (reinforces) behavior.

Positive Punishment (+P) — Anything added (positive) *(that your dog doesn't like)* that *decreases* (punishes) behavior.

Negative Reinforcement (-R) — Anything taken away (negative) *(that your dog doesn't like)* that *increases* (reinforces) behavior.

Negative Punishment (-P) — Anything taken away (negative) *(that your dog likes)* that *decreases* (punishes) behavior.

a "mistake." If you use positive reinforcement, you will have a more positive mind-set.

For instance, it is absolutely impossible to teach a dog "don't." Don't pull on leash, don't jump on strangers, don't chase the deer, don't, don't, *don't*. On the other hand, it is incredibly easy to teach a dog "do." Do walk calmly by my side, do sit politely for petting, do come instantly when I call. This may seem like a subtle and negligible difference, these do's versus don'ts. It is subtle, but oh so important! If you are always focused on what you *don't* want your dog to do, you may lose sight of the real picture— what you want your dog to do *instead*. Once you have your do's in place, you'll be able to fix any problem that comes down the pike. You want your dog to be as successful as possible, and your training should be geared to that end goal. Failure is a poor teacher. Although in positive training you always try to set the dog up to be right, there will be times when a dog will give a "wrong" response. Don't be in a hurry to "correct" him. Give him a few seconds to THINK. Only by sampling other behaviors can your dog find what exactly gets him reinforcement. In positive training, failure is not necessarily bad—instead it teaches the dog what works and what doesn't.

By adding something your dog enjoys to increase desired behavior, you are creating an upbeat learning experience and instilling a desire to learn that nothing surpasses. A dog that willingly offers behaviors, loves to think and loves to learn is a joy to behold. Seeing a handler learn to break behaviors down into manageable pieces for his dog and recognize even the smallest successes is sheer delight.

It took my Sheltie six years to overcome his fear that I would hurt him if he made a mistake. Even though he no longer shuts down and does try very hard to learn new things, he still doesn't pick up new behaviors as quickly as my two other dogs that were positively trained from the beginning.

Unfortunately, desired behaviors are not the only behaviors that can be positively reinforced. It is easy to inadvertently positively reinforce unwanted behaviors, also.

- Your dog is aggressing; you kneel down and pet him in what you think is a reassuring manner and he aggresses even more.
- Your dog is barking at you to "hurry up and feed me"; you hurry up and feed him and his pushy behavior increases.

If you have made errors similar to these in the past, they are easily fixable. Once you define your cue-behavior-consequence pattern, you'll be able to rectify the problem using positive reinforcement.

Positive Punishment

Your dog is barking and the citronella collar is activated. His barking may decrease. Your dog is pulling on leash, so you yank him back until he stops pulling. You have added something to the environment to decrease his behavior; you used positive punishment. Good job, huh? *No.* I do *not* advocate positive punishment—in fact, I highly recommend that you stay away from it. Why would I say this, when it certainly *seems* to be working? After all, your dog stopped barking and stopped pulling. Well, let's look at how you "solved" these undesired behaviors a little more closely.

Let's start with the first example. Okay, your dog is barking...at what? Is he barking at wildlife, shadows, another dog or person, you? Why is he barking? There are five reasons why dogs bark:

- Excitement of the moment—He is overaroused by the sight of something or someone.
- Fear—He barks when alone, in stress or redirection.
- Learned behavior—He has been reinforced with attention for barking in the past.
- Defense/guard—His bark is used as a warning, perhaps with growling first.
- Frustration—He barks at being tied up alone. This can be stereotypic and include such behaviors as digging and self-mutilation.

None of these reasons for barking would be helped by punishment. You turn on the citronella collar or spray him with water (*positive = something added*) and he stops barking (*punishment = behavior decreased*). Has he *learned* to stop barking? Has he learned that being quiet is more reinforcing than barking? What he has learned is that when the collar is on his neck—when that threat of punishment is there—he had better tow the line. What if he were barking at something he was afraid of? He may now make the association that icky stuff gets squirted in his face and mouth whenever he sees the scary thing. Will this help him get over his fear? It would be more productive to change his association with the scary thing than to simply stop his reaction (barking).

Let's say you are claustrophobic and just the thought of being in an elevator is enough to make you perspire. It really doesn't make any difference to you that millions of people safely ride elevators each day. Nor does it change your feelings knowing that all those millions emerge intact. You are scared—period. Forcing you onto an elevator will not alleviate your fear.

Similarly, your dog is afraid of something and aggresses. If he is hurt in the process of your trying to stop him from aggressing, will he feel better or worse about the scary thing? Now his initial fear response to that stimulus has probably increased in intensity, now perhaps the sight of a spray bottle makes him cringe. It is far more beneficial to transform the stimulus from a scary one into one where wonderful things happen to him.

Your dog continually pulls on the leash. You continually yank him back (*positive = something added*). Pain is felt in his neck, trachea and spine when he pulls and stops when he stays at your side (*punishment = behavior decreases*). Pain is being paired with you and possibly with any provoking stimulus that is around. As a possible side effect, you may be teaching your dog to be leash aggressive. Plus, he has not really learned to enjoy walking nicely by your side.

Animals in the wild learn almost all they know from positive punishment. The effects of this dictate and shape their behaviors and how they live. It is probably safe to say that we all realize and accept that wild animals—bear, big cats, etc.—can and will attack when any threat, real or perceived, is presented. Having their behavior molded by positive punishment creates animals that display aggressive and unpredictable tendencies. They live their lives always on alert, ready to defend themselves and their resources. Behold the power of positive punishment! Wild animals need to be on edge to survive; your dog doesn't.

Negative Reinforcement

This type of training strengthens or increases a behavior because a negative condition is stopped or avoided as a consequence of the behavior.

Negative reinforcement increases a behavior by taking something away that the dog doesn't like, thus increasing the likelihood that, under similar circumstances, the behavior will occur again in the future.

It is relieving (reinforcing) for the dog to get away from anything he may find unpleasant: the vet, a dog, a person, a leash pop, whatever.

Therefore, any action by the dog that enables him to escape pain or discomfort is reinforced by the relief he experiences. If your dog growls at you when you try to groom him and you stop, his growling while grooming will increase.

Many traditional trainers use the ear pinch to teach their dogs to retrieve a dumbbell. This is how it goes: The dog's ear is pinched hard enough to elicit a scream and an open mouth from the dog (positive punishment—pain being added) and then released once the dog takes the dumbbell (negative reinforcement—pain stopped). The dog has a few choices of how to react in the future. He may take the dumbbell really fast to avoid the pain, he may run away the next time he sees the dumbbell, or he may freak out if someone innocently tries to pet his ears.

I try very hard not to anthropomorphize—turning dogs into people and people into dogs—but I do think that we can have a better understanding of our dogs with a little thought experiment.

Let's say you get a job in a foreign country and you don't know the customs or the language. Your new employers find it unbelievable that you don't speak the language; they constantly nitpick, yell and otherwise berate you for not understanding what is expected of you. You do not understand what they are saying, but you know they are unhappy and you are miserable. You can't quit and there are no interpreters to tell you what your employers want.

Yes, I know this is ridiculous and you wouldn't actually get a job in a foreign country if you didn't know the language. But similarly, your dog does not speak English and you do not speak dog. In terms of negative reinforcement, you have three choices of how to react to the behavior of your employers. Your dog has the same three choices in reaction to your negative reinforcement. You or your dog may run away (escape), become very shy or just sit in a frozen position (avoidance), or lash out whenever your boss/trainer/owner comes near in an effort to get him to stay away (aggress).

Negative reinforcement differs from the other three "consequences," in that it is usually further divided into two components, *escape* and *avoidance*.

Escape means the behavior *lessens* the existing aversiveness. In other words, something offensive is happening to the dog and he escapes to stop it. You continually use positive punishment or negative reinforcement to train your dog, and the first chance he gets, he runs away. This is *escape*. The dog was actually experiencing the aversive stimulus, and the response terminated it.

Avoidance means the behavior *prevents* an impending unpleasant circumstance. In other words, the dog can see that something offensive is going to happen to him and he avoids it. Your dog won't come inside because he knows you are going to put him in the crate and leave him alone for eight hours. I stay away from foods with yeast, because if I don't, I feel faint and nauseous. There was a *threat* of an aversive stimulus—getting sick from eating yeast—but the *response*—not eating yeast—prevented its onset. (Of course, there are times when I say "to heck with the nausea, I am going to eat a bagel," but that's another story.)

What escape and avoidance have in common is that both are instances of behavior leading to an improvement in the environment (hence the behavior is reinforced) by removing (therefore negative) some amount of the aversiveness of the environment. As is always the case with reinforcement, life is better for the behavior having occurred, thus increasing the probability that the behavior will recur in the future under similar circumstances.

Negative Punishment

Negative punishment is the punishment option of choice for positive trainers. The dog's behavior removes (negative) something desirable from the environment, thereby decreasing the occurrence of that behavior (punishment) in the future. Physical pain doesn't necessarily come into play here. Often, the consequence of the behavior is that the dog loses something of value. Your dog may lose his opportunity to play or eat yummy treats.

My Border Collie Beau thought competition stays were a waste of time (yes, he told me so). To fix this problem, if he broke his stay, I calmly and quickly put him in his crate (meaning he did not have the opportunity to play once the stay was complete) (negative). I then brought out one of my other dogs and, while Beau watched, played with his favorite toy. If Beau remained in his stay, I added the "big guns" in terms of the best reinforcers—swimming, Frisbee playing and tug (positive reinforcement). As a result, Beau's "getting up while doing a stay" behavior decreased (punishment).

Your dog jumps on you or is being pushy and you walk away, thus withholding the attention he wants. His jumping/pushy behavior will decrease. If you also positively reinforce for "calm, not jumping, not pushy" behaviors, the unwanted actions will decrease faster.

As you can see, using positive reinforcement and negative punishment will create an eager, happy, willing dog that experiences a minimum of toxic side effects in all areas of his life.

Another point to keep in mind about punished behavior is that it occurs because, most likely, it was reinforced in the past. Your dog got attention by jumping and being pushy (in a completely unofficial, undocumented study, I have observed that 40 percent of all people will pet a jumping dog: "It's okay, I have dogs"), in the same way that we all have gotten somewhere faster (we have been reinforced) by speeding.

The downside of punishment is that it leads to finer discrimination—most of us remember where we got our last speeding ticket and we never speed in that location again, although we may speed elsewhere. Your dog may not chew inappropriate objects while you are in the room, but as soon as you leave, he is eating razor blades or your favorite shoes.

Perhaps in the past you have done the same things over and over again, each time expecting a different result. You punished your dog and kept punishing, regardless of the fact that it did not change his behavior for the better. You influence your dog every moment you interact with him. If you have made some of the mistakes listed in this and previous chapters and got behaviors you didn't want—well, now you know why. Once you understand the why, you can easily fix the problem by changing your behavior.

POINTS TO PONDER

❖ *Classical conditioning takes a neutral stimulus and pairs it with a reflexive action, such as drooling, excitement or fear. It is important that all of your dog's interactions with previously meaningless things are pleasant ones—otherwise the dog may make an association that you don't like.*

❖ *When training, there are three components to teaching any behavior: antecedent (cue), behavior and consequence. All behaviors have consequences—some of which can be good and some of which can be unpleasant. Some consequences increase behavior and some decrease behavior. Although some consequences may seem to decrease unwanted behaviors, there often is a price to pay in terms of possible bad associations and increased inappropriate behaviors.*

Counterconditioning and Desensitization

It is important that you understand something about the science of behavioral psychology and how it relates to dog aggression and its remedies. This will make a huge difference in how successful you will be in helping your aggressive dog. The goal here is to make sure you do not become a puppet, following blindly what others say, without real understanding of the methodology. If you understand the science behind the method, you will be able to use your own judgment when new situations arise.

One of the most important things to recognize is that *every time* you take your dog out into the world, you are training him. You must make sure that each experience he has is positive and does not cause him undue stress. You will need to totally control all of his experiences; no willy-nilly mingling allowed lest the dog have a negative experience. Your goal is to set up a positive association that will work to countercondition your dog to the situation he finds frightening. You want this to be done at a low stress level that will desensitize your dog to the scary stimulus. If you take your dog out into a situation that he is not ready to handle with calm assurance, you will *sensitize* him to that situation, setting up more negative associations and making his aggression worse.

Finding just the right level of stimulation for your dog at any given level in his training is an art, and you should not feel bad if you make a mistake and your dog occasionally becomes overaroused. We all make mistakes, but the lesson must be learned!

Socialization should be done with young pups to prevent aggression, *not* with dogs that already are aggressive. Exposing an already reactive dog to the triggers that set him off, without proper and gentle desensitization, will most certainly intensify his fears. His stress level will rise dramatically and instead of seeing a trend of lessening aggression, the episodes will become more severe and less discriminative.

COUNTERCONDITIONING

Counterconditioning is a type of rehabilitation based on the principles of classical conditioning (see Chapter Five). Counterconditioning works to replace bad or unpleasant emotional responses due to prior conditioning—hence the word *counter*—with more pleasant responses.

For instance, let's say you put a prong collar on your dog and yanked back every time he aggressed at another dog (positive punishment). Your dog has now *learned* that the presence of other dogs means he will feel pain. You have conditioned (taught) him to fear other dogs, and most likely he will continue to aggress at other dogs, given the chance. Similarly, if you let people knee your dog in the chest when he jumps up on them (positive punishment), he will associate strangers with pain, and will be conditioned to fear strangers. He may very well begin to aggress at people. Every time a bad thing happens to a dog around particular stimuli, you create the potential for aggression.

Even if you aren't physically or verbally punishing, by constantly exposing him to the scary bad things without a plan of action, you may be giving him more reasons to be afraid.

Counterconditioning is all about reducing the intensity of a conditioned (learned) response (such as anxiety or aggression) by teaching incompatible responses (such as relaxation or other behaviors) to the scary bad things.

To countercondition your dog's behavior of biting people or dogs, you can pair pleasant and positive things for the dog in the presence of these stimuli (positive reinforcement), so that they actually become a cue that good things are going to happen.

THE PROCESS: DESENSITIZATION

Systematic desensitization is a lot like dieting. The most effective way to take off the pounds and keep them off is to go slowly—one pound at a time. However, by nature, we humans like to see immediate results, so we crash diet, starve ourselves and follow countless other diet fads. Yes, you may see quicker results, but the percentage of people who bounce back to their starting weight, or even heavier, is astounding. Additionally, in the process, we can experience all kinds of unhealthy side effects.

In the late 1950s, a researcher named Joseph Wolpe (1915-1997) developed a treatment program for anxiety that was based on the principles of counterconditioning. Wolpe found that anxiety symptoms could be reduced when the anxiety-producing stimuli were presented in a careful and controlled manner while being methodically paired with a relaxation response (positive reinforcement). This came to be known as systematic desensitization.

Systematic desensitization is a methodology designed to treat people and animals that experience extreme anxiety about specific events, situations, things or people. The approaches for both people and dogs are quite similar and entail designing a program of slowly increasing anxiety-provoking situations, and, for people, learning relaxation techniques or, for dogs, learning alternate and incompatible behaviors. The entire fearful event first is broken down into its smallest components. Then, beginning at the bottom, or least scary, step, those components are associated with relaxation and alternate behaviors.

It is important to realize that there are very real physiological processes going on in a dog's body (and yours for that matter) during stress and any aggressive action. By beginning at the bottom or the least scary situation, and moving step by step slowly and carefully, you will be able to avoid many of the hormonal changes that can exacerbate the problem. Rush the process and look out! Hormonal overload and stress-related diseases are just waiting for your dog.

HORMONES DON'T LIE

There are many different hormones that help your dog deal with the stress at hand and keep him safe from danger. These hormones help him mobilize his body for a flight or fight response; they control and are controlled by each and every organ in his body, and determine whether he can eat, drink, procreate and even how thick his blood is at any given moment.

So what does this have to do with aggression?

There are two parts of the autonomic nervous system (ANS). The sympathetic nervous system is the "action" part of the ANS. It prepares the body to either fight or flee from danger, whether real or imagined. It produces alertness, arousal, and muscle tension in preparation for action, and inhibits salivation and digestion, accelerates the heartbeat, and primes the endocrine system for the secretion of certain stress hormones such as adrenaline. Many of these hormones even blunt physical pain—the dog can't be worrying about his injury yet, he still needs to continue fighting for his life.

The parasympathetic nervous system takes over when your dog is calm, to help him perform relaxing tasks—eat, sleep, or chew on a bone. In addition, the parasympathetic nervous system supports growth and energy storage—activities exactly the opposite from those the sympathetic nervous system allows. The sympathetic and parasympathetic nervous systems cannot be turned on at the same time. It's all or nothing with these two parts of the ANS. Your dog cannot chow down a huge meal while running for his life.

There are many different stress hormones released by the endocrine system that work hand in hand with the sympathetic nervous system. All are important and fascinating in how they help your dog's body cope when under stress. Two of them in particular—epinephrine (the more common term is adrenaline) and glucocorticoids—are an amazingly versatile bunch of hormones. They do three incredible things: (1) they activate the body to deal with a present danger, (2) they help the body recover from the stress, and (3) they prepare the body for the next stressor. This way, your dog isn't taken unaware by more dangers coming down the pike. Different amounts of adrenaline and glucocorticoids are released depending on the intensity of the stressor your dog encounters. Based on the severity of the reaction, these hormones (and others) will take anywhere from two to six full days to come back down to normal.

Adrenaline works faster than glucocorticoids (both hereafter are called by the generic term of "hormones") and acts like a fast rush (an adrenaline rush, so to speak). During an extreme anxiety response (aggression), your dog is trying to cope, trying to keep himself safe, but he may be doing this in wildly ineffectual ways (especially if the fear is imagined), utilizing many contradictory coping responses all at once, and might not notice when the threat is over. You may have seen your dog flailing, lunging and barking wildly at his provoking stimuli, so completely out of control that even when the stimulus is no longer in sight, his behavior remains the same. In fact, he may start to view everything and anything as a continued threat to his safety.

One of my students, a Boxer mix named Champie, loves people and dislikes other animals immensely. When we brought her out by herself to work on some foundation behaviors, she started reacting in a frenzied and uncontrolled manner, even though there were no dogs around.

Picture this fairly common human example: You just miss getting into a car accident. Hormones have energized your body to avoid the danger. Once you are safe, you feel your stress hormones pumping and your heart racing, preparing your body for the next danger. A few minutes go by and you start to relax, feeling relieved that the danger was averted. Now your hormones are helping your body to recover from the stress response. Then whammo! Another car swerves in front of you— another near miss. Your hormone levels are even higher now because they didn't have a chance to come back down to normal. Your heart races even faster.

As Robert Sapolsky writes in his fascinating book, *Why Zebras Don't Get Ulcers*, "Together, glucocorticoids and secretions of the sympathetic nervous system (epinephrine and norepinephrine) account for a large percentage of what happens in your body during stress. These are the workhorses of the stress-response." In addition he states, "Glucocorticoids, glucagon and the sympathetic nervous system raise circulating levels of sugar glucose—as we will see, these hormones are essential for mobilizing energy during stress."

This last statement says it all—one thing you *don't* need in your aggressive dog is for him to be constantly "mobilizing energy," thus having his sympathetic nervous system (fight-or-flight system) in high gear all of the time. I'll be addressing this concept again in a moment.

Let's go back to the car crash scenario for a second. Your heart is racing faster and a myriad of stress hormones are coursing through your body. Then another car and yet another cut in front of you. There is no way you can pull off the road and no way you can stop these idiot drivers from trying to kill you! You are now so sensitized to cars coming toward you that you may become more "proactive," driving more aggressively yourself. (This is why, if I have to go into New York City, I take the train or bus.)

Similarly, because of the constant flow of hormones due to the many stress-inducing events, your dog's body may never get a chance to come

People who suffer phobias know that exposure to their object of fear can be crippling. Humans can understand, to a certain extent, the basis of their fears and seek professional help. Your dog cannot do these things—he has to rely on you to understand and aid him in overcoming his learned fears.

back down to a normal and relaxed state. Such chronic stress can cause the dog to overreact with aggressive displays *faster and with more intensity and less perceived provocation.*

As part of the desensitization process, it is important to remember that the sympathetic nervous system and the parasympathetic nervous system cannot be turned on a the same time. Your dog cannot be nervous/afraid and relaxed at the same time, so it is imperative that you put the dog in situations where he can be relaxed. If his fight-or-flight system is in gear, he will not be able to be calm around his provoking stimuli.

Danger Ahead—Road Flooded

Flooding is a prolonged and forced exposure to a stimulus that is or has become noxious (terrifying or frightening). Flooding is based on the premise that when a patient escapes from an anxiety-provoking experience, that anxiety is actually reinforced through conditioning. Anxiety is extinguished by exposing the patient to the feared stimuli with no chance of escape. The patient must remain in the fear-producing situation until he adjusts and is no longer anxious. Flooding is the quickest form of treatment for phobias; however, it is very difficult to obtain patient willingness due to the extremely aversive (punishing) nature of this process.

Truly effective methods of modifying behavior or treating canine aggression are based on the studies of behavior and scientific research. However, this should not be taken as a blanket license to utilize all methods condoned for use in humans. Flooding is one technique that isn't recommended for treating a reactive dog. Promoting the experience of anxiety is not a helpful procedure when working with your dog. He won't just "get over it" when forcibly exposed to his own personal scary bad thing. Flooding is the direct opposite of systematic desensitization.

There is an important aspect of this technique that prevents it from being helpful in treating dogs. Even with people, getting a patient's consent is difficult because flooding is so harsh. Humans, of course, have the tremendous advantage of total awareness of what will transpire during therapy, since it is discussed and explained to them in detail. "Exposure" in flooding can be real (actually being in the presence of, seeing, touching, etc.) or imagined (visualized). I know of no way to use any common language to explain and describe to a dog what is about to happen. Systematic desensitization, if executed properly, is safer and has less risk of "fallout"—that is, less risk of eliciting aggressive responses of greater intensity and duration.

POINTS TO PONDER

❧ *Any negative interaction with your dog's feared object will intensify his aggression.*

❧ *Socialization is for young dogs; desensitization and counterconditioning are for the already aggressive dog.*

❧ *Counterconditioning is all about making sure good things now happen around your dog's scary things.*

❧ *Desensitization is all about carefully and slowly setting up situations in which your dog will not have an aggressive response.*

7 The Starting Point: Ten Foundation Behaviors

One of the keys in the desensitization process is to train your dog to perform alternate and incompatible behaviors that are in direct conflict with aggressing. An untrained dog is one that will aggress at the drop of a hat because he doesn't know what to do *instead*. By teaching him all kinds of behaviors, he will focus his mind and body on you, rather than the thing he normally aggresses toward. For all of the behaviors listed in this book, I have discussed how to train them using positive reinforcement techniques. It is vital that you set your dog up to be right. If he does make a mistake, please do not fall back into using positive punishment (adding something he doesn't like, to decrease behavior) or negative reinforcement (taking something away that your dog doesn't like, to increase behavior). This will only confuse or stress him out and possibly incite him to aggress.

Barbara came to me with three unruly dogs. Aggression was starting between them in certain situations. We worked on training all three dogs using positive reinforcement to the same level, teaching them simple foundation behaviors and the budding aggression problem just simply stopped.

The greater part of all mischief in the world arises from the fact that men do not sufficiently understand their own aims. They have undertaken to build a tower, and spend no more labor on the foundation than would be necessary to erect a hut.

—Johann Wolfgang von Goethe (1749–1832)

73

Some of the behaviors listed in this and the following chapter are vital, and some are just plain fun. The more alternatives your dog has, the better off you will be. Both your dog's life and your own will be enriched because of them. If these behaviors seem a bit picky—well, they are. Aggressive dogs need to be trained to a higher level than "normal" dogs because of the desensitization process.

I run an "On the Road" class, where I take the group to a few different locations to train—parking lots, trails and parks. A dog from my aggressive dog class was there during one such session, and she proved to be the most well-trained of the group. Why? Because she had to be better trained. She displayed unfailing attention to her handler and was not easily distracted by the environment.

The behaviors given here are divided into two sections: why you need that behavior and how to train it. Each behavior should first be trained in a low distraction area, and then you can move on to working around more distractions. I understand that your dog is aggressive and that this may be difficult to do without setting the dog up to aggress. At the end of Chapter Eight are the how-to's of distraction-training your aggressive dog.

IS YOUR FOUNDATION MADE OF STRAW OR BRICK?

Foundation behaviors are the first line of defense against aggression. Most problem behaviors stem from inadequate or nonexistent training. Complete attention on you, as well as a correct response to simple but important cues, is a must before you can start your retraining program. As animal behaviorist Ted Turner states, "Ninety percent of all complex behavioral problems can be linked back to a poor foundation."

There are a few phases of foundation behaviors that you can draw upon to help you and your dog stay focused. I will discuss each of them in detail in this chapter and then will describe exactly how to utilize them in Chapters Eight and Nine.

BEHAVIOR NUMBER ONE: BRIDGE RESPONSE

Why You Need It

A bridge is what tells the dog that he did something right the instant he does it. A bridge can be a clicker or a certain word (such as "yes!").

Why are bridges important? In order for the dog to connect the behavior he performed with the reinforcer you dole out, it must be delivered within about one-half second of the desired behavior. With some behaviors, this is entirely possible. For instance, when training a "sit," you can very likely predict the exact time the dog's hind end will greet the ground. If you are prepared, you can certainly deliver the reinforcer within a half second. However, there are some behaviors where it may be physically impossible for you to get the reinforcer to the dog within that very short time period. A good example is the drop on recall, where the dog is some distance from you when he performs the correct behavior. The marker then bridges the time between behavior and reinforcer. (The marker itself becomes what is called a secondary reinforcer.)

Why is your dog's response to the bridge important? Because if he doesn't recognize that he did something right, he won't do it again. In this book, I will be calling the bridge "click" with the treat or other reward as the consequence, and I will refer to the click and treat sequence as "c/t."

How to Train It
Piece of cake! Just remember classical conditioning. For one session, cut up treats into tiny pieces. Get a clicker. "Prime" the clicker by clicking and then, within one-half second, feeding your dog a treat. Count out sixty treats and repeat the above step. This exercise teaches the dog to make the association that "click" means he did something right and that he gets reinforced. You likely won't have to repeat this exercise. However, if your dog isn't making the connection right away, don't worry. Just do it again for another session or two. You can use the same pattern if you use a verbal bridge. Say "yes!" and then treat within a half second. We talk to and around our dogs all of the time; most of the time they hear "blahblahblah" since dogs are not naturally a verbal species. So if you use a verbal bridge, you will need to do this for more than sixty repetitions.

BEHAVIOR NUMBER TWO: EYE CONTACT

Why You Need It
If your dog is looking at you adoringly at all times, he can't be staring at the scary bad thing. Eye contact is the basis of any other behavior you may want to teach your dog, so don't skimp on this.

Dog giving eye contact to his owner. Photo by P. Dennison.

How to Train It

Paired with food and the clicker, eye contact becomes a powerful reinforcer for the dog. Plus, you can't teach the dog anything if he isn't paying attention to you.

1. Stand and wait passively for your dog to look at your face (have your hands down by your side). Be forewarned—he may try to mug your hands and snatch the treats. Ignore any attempts by him to obtain the treats.

2. The instant he looks at you, click and treat.

3. Continue for a few minutes. After a day or two, he should be boring holes in your head and you will not have to c/t all of the time. You can periodically add some praise and play instead of the c/t.

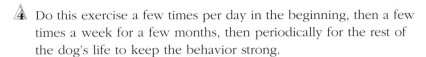

4. Do this exercise a few times per day in the beginning, then a few times a week for a few months, then periodically for the rest of the dog's life to keep the behavior strong.

5. Play this game at first with no distractions and gradually add in more and more distractions, making sure to practice in at least ten to fifteen new safe locations per month. You will need your dog to focus on you in any and all situations.

BEHAVIOR NUMBER THREE: NAME RECOGNITION

Why You Need It

If your dog does happen to glance away or get loose, instant name response is a "must have" behavior. Your goal is to have your dog whip his head in your direction the moment you say his name.

How to Train It

You will add name recognition to the eye contact equation. Wait for your dog to look at you, say his name and then c/t. Don't say his name to get him to look at you—say his name *because* he is looking at you. One way is nagging and the other way is training. Repeat billions of times because you really want your dog to respond instantly to his name (with whiplash!). Practice this along with eye contact a few times per day to start, then a few times per week, and then sporadically for the rest of the dog's life.

BEHAVIOR NUMBER FOUR: HEEL ON A LOOSE LEASH

Why You Need It

Why do I say, "heel" instead of "walk" on a loose leash? If your dog is just walking on lead, he could be looking anywhere and at anything—deer poo, squirrels, birds, kids, dogs, people, gopher holes, bicycles, et cetera. If your dog is heeling, he should be looking up at you 100 percent of the time unless you give him permission to do otherwise. Just as with the stationary eye contact, if he is looking at you, he won't be staring at the scary things.

Before you train your dog to heel, it is helpful to understand why dogs pull on leash in the first place:

- ❖ The number one reason—We follow, so they learn that to get where they want to go, they have to pull.
- ❖ The number two reason—Opposition reflex, a natural reflexive action, causes them to push or pull against anything that is pushing or pulling against them.
- ❖ The number three reason—Dogs are thinking about what they are looking at. If they aren't looking at you, then you can pretty much guess they aren't thinking about you either.

So, what is the answer? Teach your dog that to look at you and to heel (either side is fine, although if you are considering competition obedience or Rally, the left side should be more heavily reinforced) "pays off." Heel position is going to become the "kitchen" for your dog.

How to Train It

Start with behavior number two—eye contact in a stationary position. Once your dog is actively counting your eyelashes, you can progress to giving attention while moving.

1   Use a long line of fifteen to fifty feet or work off leash if you have a safe, fenced-in area. If your dog willingly stays with you on a long line, it will be easier to teach him to stay with you willingly on a short line. The standard six-foot leash *forces* him to be next to you, which you do not want. You want him to be able to make the correct choice and then you will reinforce him for making that choice. Additionally, if your dog is pulling, it hurts his neck. He will learn to associate the pain of the tight collar with you and will struggle even more to get away, increasing his opposition reflex. When you start out with this behavior in place, my recommendation would be to put a harness on your dog—that way, if he does hit the end of it, he won't be doing any neck, spinal or tracheal damage.

Begin teaching this behavior with mild distractions only, until you and your dog get the hang of it. Walk backwards, so that the dog follows you. After each step, c/t without stopping your backward movement. Don't lure him with your hands; otherwise, he is only learning to follow your hands. Just move and he should follow.

Jim doing moving backups, while Molly is following him. Molly is wearing an X-Back sledding harness. Photo by P. Dennison.

2 At first, c/t each step, then once your dog is focused on you, start to move erratically to the right and left, not just in straight lines, making sure you c/t him for following you. Dogs love sudden movements—it will help him stay with you if you are a bit unpredictable. If your dog is moving past you, stand still and wait for him to come back to you. Don't let him pull you and don't you pull him—just lock your arms and bend your knees, keep your weight low and he won't pull you off your feet. If you insist on calling him, don't use his name (until he has fantastic name response); use "hey you," "earth to puppy," "hellllooooooo"—if he isn't going to respond, you don't want to teach him that his name is "white noise." Once you have his attention back on you, move in fun ways and *then* c/t him for paying attention to you. After one to two training sessions, only c/t if he is looking up at your face.

It is very important to keep up the high value of your dog's name and not dilute it; that is, you shouldn't repeat his name continually when he has no intention of responding. In the beginning stages, be sure to only say his name when you are pretty sure he will respond to it.

Caveat: If you reinforce the dog the instant he comes back to you, you are reinforcing the "pull, come back get a treat, pull again, come back get a treat" behavior chain. So, when the dog does come back, get at least three to five steps of attention before reinforcing.

3. Add distractions. Start with mild distractions and gradually add in harder ones. Continue to back up, moving erratically, changing directions and reinforcing the dog heavily for following you. The harder the distraction, the more valuable the reinforcer must be. Food doesn't always work and many dogs will ignore a piece of steak when confronted with the incredibly exciting smells of deer and squirrels or with their provoking stimuli. Predictability kills behavior, so it is your job to be *un*predictable, not only in how you reinforce, but in the schedule of reinforcement as well. Don't get stuck on reinforcing the same number of steps on a regular schedule. It is boring for the dog and he will return to ignoring you and pulling on leash or aggressing.

Using other reinforcers: Playing with a toy. Photo by J. Petersen.

Using other reinforcers: Plucking grass and throwing it up in the air. Photo by P. Dennison.

You have now kept your dog's attention while backing up, with a myriad of distractions and used most or all of the reinforcers listed above. Now you and he need to learn to walk in the same direction.

4 In this step, you learn the heel position, a.k.a. the Kitchen. This is the moment you've been waiting for—both of you walking forward as a team! Start your session by backing up to ensure that your dog is focused on you. Pivot to your right so that the dog comes up on your left and instantly c/t. Take another step or two and c/t. Repeat dozens of times, heavily reinforcing (using the list above) this new position. Use your left hand to feed. Although this may sound a tad anal—dictating which hand to hold the treat in—there really is good reason! If your dog is on the left and you feed with your right hand, he will move in front to get closer to the food hand and trip you.

If the dog goes ahead of you, start to move erratically, saying his name as you turn away from him. Be sure to *not* pop

Pivot to heel, so the dog is on your left. Photo by A. Kelly.

Reinforcing the dog for attention walking. Photo by A. Kelly.

him on the collar (positive punishment) when changing direction. Since he has found following you fun, he should stay with you. If he doesn't, just stand still and wait for him to re-engage with you. Then go back to being silly and reinforce him after a few steps of attention.

In case you haven't noticed, I haven't asked you to name this behavior yet. Why? Heeling is a duration behavior (as opposed to an instant behavior, like a sit) and if you name a duration behavior before it is reliable, you will be naming the sub-standard behavior and that is the behavior you will get. If your dog is pulling and you say, "heel," you have just named the pulling behavior "heel."

Once your dog is reliably staying with you, then name the behavior. "Strut," "with me," "heel," "let's go," and "walk," are the most common cue words for heeling. Don't use "come on"—you will dilute your "come" word.

On average, it takes a few weeks to teach your dog to heel. Younger dogs take less time, because they don't have a strong history of pulling. If you have an older dog, you may want to change to a harness. My favorite harnesses are listed in Appendix 2. This way, if you are of the old school and can't seem to stop popping your dog, at least you won't be hurting his neck. You can wean off of these harnesses to a buckle collar after a few weeks or you can just keep using them.

BEHAVIOR NUMBER FIVE: ACCEPT TOUCHING

Why You Need It

Being able to be handled for grooming or petting is very important and a "skill" that many dogs lack. Some dogs dislike being touched due to bad experiences, and some just naturally don't like handling of any kind. It is also important that your dog allow strangers to handle him; he may encounter many people in his life who will have to do so—veterinarians, groomers, the boarding kennel and Animal Control if he gets lost. For those of you with human-aggressive dogs, just the thought of this may give you the shakes and you may start to hyperventilate. Touch can also become a powerful reinforcer for your dog; even if he doesn't like it at first, persevere—it will become worth the effort. For those of you that have dogs that love handling (including toenail clipping) and petting, thank your lucky stars and skip to the next behavior, but remember not to take it for granted! Always reinforce appropriate behaviors.

How to Train It

Start slowly! The key for this exercise is to stay within the dog's comfort level. Some dogs are more touch sensitive than others or have different kinds of touching that they are at ease with or nervous about. Start with classical conditioning—pair food with any kind of light touching. If you can get someone to help you by clicking if the dog doesn't move away, so much the better.

1 Touch lightly under his chin and feed a treat at the same time.

2 Repeat the above step for each body part—chin, side of face, top of head, ears, snout, chest, withers, back, belly, legs, feet, tail, hind end—always a gentle touch and reinforce for no movement away from you or aggression toward you. It may take days, weeks or even months for your dog to be comfortable with these gentle strokes.

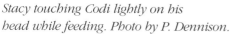

Stacy touching Codi lightly on his head while feeding. Photo by P. Dennison.

Stacy touching Codi dog lightly on his chest while feeding. Photo by P. Dennison.

Stacy touching Codi lightly on the side of his face while feeding. Photo by P. Dennison.

Cynthia touching Boomer's feet while feeding. Photo by P. Dennison.

3. Once he is accepting of the light touches, start to wean him from the treats. Touch him two or three times in a row and then feed him. Continue in this vein until your dog is actively seeking your touch and you no longer need to reinforce him for allowing the contact.

4. Always end the petting with a treat—try not to treat first and then pet. You need to make sure touching is valuable for your dog, and the order in which the treat is delivered is important. If you treat first and then pet, you are teaching your dog that petting is a signal that no more food is coming and he will work to avoid any kind of touching.

As when training other behaviors, remember that the "treat" doesn't have to be an actual piece of food. If your dog is ball or toy happy, touch gently, click for no movement away and release him to get the toy. This can actually work to your benefit; throwing the toy and having the dog chase it may lessen his stress about the handling. Call him back, reinforce for the recall, and repeat the exercise.

Approach any tactile issue—toenail clipping, brushing, grooming, bathing (which may include allowing himself to be picked up, depending on your own size and that of your dog)—the same way, following the above steps.

Slow and steady wins this race. Make it valuable and rewarding for the dog to be touched and handled and be sure to keep the sessions short—from ten to thirty seconds in length, with one to four repetitions per session. You can repeat the session many times per day.

You can also teach your dog a "settle," where he lies down on his side and you gently touch him and reward him for allowing it. This is must-have behavior, needed when checking for rashes, fleas and ticks or removing burrs or other sticky objects.

Owner picking up her puppy, while a friend feeds a treat. Photo by P. Dennison.

Stacy teaching Gwen to "settle." Photo by P. Dennison.

It took me a full year of working with Shadow, my human-aggressive Border Collie, for me to be able to safely and comfortably clip his toenails and handle, groom and bathe him without help. I never pushed it and thus never got bit—a good selling point for going slow. Shadow now enjoys grooming and handling so much that I can use them as reinforcers.

BEHAVIOR NUMBER SIX: ACCEPT SECONDARY REINFORCERS

Why You Need It

Primary reinforcers are food, water and access to sex. Dogs don't need to learn to love/need these things—they are born with an innate desire or need for them. Anything other than these three things is called a *secondary reinforcer*—touch, toys, praise, play, anything else you can think up. It is important to build your reinforcement repertoire because food pales after a while. Also, if you train using food alone, then your dog will only work for food. You will get better attention and focus if you are unpredictable in how you reinforce. To quote Ted Turner, "Be Ronald McDonald, Bozo the Clown and Howdy Doody all rolled into one."

In the beginning of training and the desensitization process, using food to reinforce appropriate behaviors is the way to go. Because you are going for calmness when provoking stimuli are around, I wouldn't recommend play and toys. "Good" arousal can quickly turn to "bad" arousal. Chasing after a Frisbee can become "chasing the Frisbee and while I am revved up, biting that person who is standing in my way."

But once your program of desensitization is further along, and you are training alone without the presence of provoking stimuli, the sky is the limit in the use of many different types of rewards. Feel free to add the more "active" reinforcers, gradually and carefully so as not to arouse your dog beyond his capability to "cool down" quickly at any given time. Food reinforcers can be of many different types: steak, chicken, cheese, tortellini, hotdogs, sausage, homemade treats, the leftovers that no one wants, anything your dog likes. Activities such as sniffing, swimming, playing with toys, fetch, tug, chasing you, long walks in the woods, petting, brushing or cuddling are wonderful ways of reinforcing your dog. Sometimes even performing a behavior can be reinforcing to your dog. How many of your dogs love to do silly pet tricks? Shakes, high fives, rollovers, bows, spins, etc., may be utilized to reinforce a good behavior. The items mentioned under heeling can also be applied to reinforce any behavior. Silly things such as a smile, a whisper, a wink and a wave can be used—be creative!

How to Train It

Even if your dog isn't naturally fond of toys, you can teach him to like them, just like you taught him to enjoy petting,

1 Tease the dog with a squeaky toy.

2. Throw the toy a few feet and run after it along with the dog.

3. Click and treat the dog for running after the toy, being sure to toss a wad of treats right next to the toy on the ground.

4. Repeat steps 1-3 at least ten to fifteen times.

5. Now raise the bar—stop chasing and let the dog do the running on his own. If he starts to go toward the toy, c/t and then run to the toy and drop a large number of treats next to the toy while cheering and clapping.

6. Repeat step 5 until your dog is racing to the toy all on his own. Be sure to heavily reinforce each and every time he gets to the toy.

7. Raise the bar again—now you want him to nose the toy, not just race to it. Click and jackpot (jackpots are wads of food) when he does, always putting the treats on the ground next to the toy. Repeat about five to eight times.

8. The next step is to have him open his mouth. Throw the toy a few feet and after he noses it, just wait. Most likely he will nose it a few times. Watch very carefully and if he even opens his mouth a tiny bit, click and jackpot, adding in cheering and clapping.

Keep on in the same way, always making it fun for your dog and making it worth his while to pick up the toy. You can even get a plush toy, cut it open and stuff some smelly treats inside. This may seem a bit ridiculous—training your dog to like toys, but it is very worth the effort it takes. On average, it will take about a month to get your dog to be really excited about playing with toys.

BEHAVIOR NUMBER SEVEN: STAYS

Why You Need It

A core behavior that no dog should be without is the stay. Stays are often underrated, underpracticed and underutilized. Yes, they are boring. Practice them anyway. Stays are lifesavers when you are surprised by scary bad things that aren't supposed to be there. They are also useful if you see the bad thing coming toward you and you have no escape route—you can ask for a stay and heavily reinforce your dog for holding position and not reacting. The stay is also handy when living with multiple dogs—especially when you want to go out the door with one dog while leaving the others behind or if you want to load the dishwasher without the pre-wash crew trying to help. Stays are also essential for teaching door etiquette. Using the instructions below, you can train the sit, down and stand stay. All are useful at one time or another, so practice all of them.

How to Train It

1. Ask your dog to sit.

2. Say "sit" again, turn slightly away from him and instantly turn back and reinforce with a treat. If he breaks position, either as you turn away or as you feed, pause, count to three, and just start over.

3. Repeat step 2 until he is staying as if he were glued to the floor. It usually takes about ten repetitions.

4. Then do the same thing, but now take one step away and go right back and reinforce with a treat. Continue for about ten repetitions or until he is consistently staying in position.

5. Repeat step 4, now taking two steps away.

6. Continue on the same track until you can go across the room and even skip around doing jumping jacks with your dog sitting as though you stapled him to the floor.

7. Practice the above steps in many different locations, not just your living room.

You may have noticed that I haven't asked you to actually say "stay" yet. Stays are another duration behavior, like heeling. If you name the stay while the dog is still popping up, then every time you ask for a stay, your dog will break out of position. Wait until he is rock solid and then name it.

BEHAVIOR NUMBER EIGHT: RECALL (COMING WHEN CALLED)

Why You Need It

The need for this is pretty much obvious. If your dog gets loose or distracted and you have instant recall, you can get your dog out of trouble and back to being focused on you.

How to Train It

Just like you did with eye contact, start training the recall using classical conditioning.

1. Have the dog in front of you, wait for him to give you eye contact, say his name, then "come," (or whatever your recall word is), and then click and treat.

2. Repeat eight billion times.

You are not asking the dog to actually move out of position—you just want him to listen to the words and have them become extremely valuable. Do this every day about twenty times per day for a few weeks, then a few times per week for the rest of the dog's life to keep it strong.

Once the dog associates your recall word with good things, you can begin the actual training. Make sure your come signal is clear and consistent—keep the word exactly the same each and every time you say it. In the beginning stages of the recall, do not say the word unless the dog is already on his way to you. To properly teach the dog what behavior we are naming, you must pair the word with the behavior for the dog to learn exactly what "come" means. Perhaps you have already contaminated the word "come" by overusing it, and your dog thinks "come" means to "hightail it outta here." No problem! Just choose another verbal cue for your recall. Dogs don't speak English, so you can choose any word, but a good suggestion for a new word is "here."

For the recall, be as generous as you can when your dog comes to you. After all, an instant come may save his life one day. To make yourself more interesting than the environment is not an easy feat, and to develop the trust a recall demands when provoking stimuli are around is vital.

Karen brought her Dalmatian to me for training. Her come word was poisoned, so I had her change the word to "here." Within two days Tiffany was responding instantly each and every time her owner called her.

Here are some more tips on teaching the recall:

❖ Say "come" (or your recall word) only when your dog is on his way to you and you are prepared to reinforce heavily—for at least twenty seconds. If you don't have any reinforcers on you, you can run to get them, whooping and cheering, keeping your dog's attention on you.

❖ Make sure the dog comes within a few inches of you—do not reach out to feed him.

❖ Make sure that when you say "come" it doesn't sound like a machine gun, "comecomecomecomecome." Be clear, be consistent, be brief.

Search and Rejoice

Wait for your dog to be distracted or have another person occupy your dog while you quietly slip away and hide. Once you are out of sight, call your dog. If you are working with a partner, he or she should immediately drop the leash upon hearing you call your dog's name. Your helper can help to motivate your dog by excitedly asking, "Where's mommy (daddy)?! Find mommy (daddy)!" Once your dog finds you, reinforce heavily with praise, food, toys, etc. When starting out, please make sure that your dog can find you! Hide in plain sight and make the search more difficult only as your dog learns the game.

Andrea is "hiding" from Flute and Flute is racing to find her. Photo by P. Dennison.

Simon Says

"Chase me!" Encourage your dog to chase you as you run away. Make yourself enticing and interesting. Move slowly, then dart quickly—act like a bunny! Feint left and right and crouch low to the ground. When your dog catches up to you (and he surely will!) c/t. Then Simon (that's you) says "sit"—c/t. Simon says "down," and then you're off and running again! Simon says "I love you and am going to hug you!" Keep your dog guessing about what behavior you'll ask for next! If your dog knows any silly tricks, add them in randomly.

End of the Rope Recall

Go to an open area or field. Be equipped with a long line (fifty feet is great), some treats and toys. Walk along, allowing your dog to explore the world. Way *before* he reaches the end of the line, say his name. If you have done your homework, you'll have a dog with wonderful name response and he'll turn his head to look at you. When he does, ask him to come. If he does, c/t and reward heavily. Then release him to explore some more by saying something like "Okay, go play" or "Okay, go sniff." If your dog doesn't respond initially, don't worry and don't repeat yourself. Stand still and wait—he will come back eventually. You must always win in the "patience game," so don't give in. When your dog does return to you, c/t, and then release again.

I am calling Shadow to me before he hits the end of his long line. Photo by A. Kelly.

Ideally, you want to train your dog to come away from things without him thinking that his fun has ended by returning to you. If you reward for a speedy recall and then release again, he'll quickly learn that coming to you not only *doesn't* signal the end of his fun, but he gets wonderful reinforcers and is then allowed to resume exploring. You should start to see your dog checking back with you every few seconds. When he does this on his own, heavily reinforce him.

Run-Away Recall

This is a game that both you and your dog will love. Don't be surprised when your dog catches on to this really quickly. In just a few quick repetitions, you'll find it more and more difficult to outrun him.

1. Throw a treat a few feet away. (You throw the treat to distract your dog and give yourself a head start.) Make sure the dog sees it!

2. Tell your dog to "get it."

3. While he is busying himself with eating the treat, run away from him really fast! You may need to make it obvious (by stomping your feet as you retreat) that you are on the move. Your dog will inevitably begin to run towards you or chase you as you are moving away.

4. As the dog is coming to you, say "come" (pairing the word with the behavior). When he gets to you, click and treat with a jackpot. Jackpots are given for every come and are fed one treat at a time. To a dog, a single handful of food is the same as one treat, so spread them out to keep your dog with you longer! Be variable in the amount of the jackpots—ten treats, three, nine, eight, thirty, one, seven—you get the idea. Be generous! Add in some play, petting and praise.

About one quarter of the time, grab your dog's collar when he comes to you and then feed your jackpots. Any idea why you need to grab your dog's collar when he arrives? (This is a test.) How many times has your dog approached you and stopped just short of you being able to grab him? When you make that motion to grasp his collar, he's off and running, initiating that never-to-be-won-by-humans, "chase me" game. What if your dog has somehow escaped and a Good Samaritan attempts to corral him? Having a dog that is used to having his collar grabbed will make it easier and safer to catch him.

Pete is dropping a treat for Cornelia so he can get a head start at running away.

Now that Pete was able to get a head start, Cornelia races to catch up with him as Pete says, "Cornelia, come!" Photos by P. Dennison.

Stacy is grabbing Gwen's collar while feeding. Photo by P. Dennison.

BEHAVIOR NUMBER NINE: CONTROL IN AND OUT OF DOORWAYS (CAR AND BUILDINGS)

Why You Need It

This is needed simply because you may not know what is on the other side of a door. When you take your dog out of the car, it can be quite unpleasant, to say the least, if he dashes out into traffic or after the dog/person/squirrel or other provoking stimuli that you didn't happen to notice. It is imperative to have your dog's focus on you rather than the environment when entering a new location. This behavior is also useful when crossing streets or going around corners, barriers, solid fences or shrubbery, anywhere you can't see who or what is coming. Amazing what we who own aggressive dogs have to take into account, isn't it?

Stacy is having her dog stay while she looks around the corner of a building in case someone is walking by. Photo by P. Dennison.

Lori has Bo stay in the car with the door open while provoking stimuli are around. At this point in his training, this is a safe distance. Photo by P. Dennison.

Lori has Bo come out of the car and give her attention when provoking stimuli are closer. Photo by P. Dennison.

Shadow (an experienced dog at this point) exhibiting door etiquette while provoking stimuli are quite close. Photo by C. Palmer.

How to Train It

Start with a regular doorway.

1. Have your dog on leash and ask him to sit.

2. Put your hand on the doorknob.

3. If he doesn't move out of position, click and treat. If he does, just ask him to sit again.

4. Repeat steps 2 and 3 about four to five times or until your dog is comfortable with remaining in the sit stay. (You don't have to say "stay"—remember, get the behavior first and then name it.)

5. Your next step will be to turn the knob without opening the door.

6. Click and treat if your dog doesn't move out of position. If he does, just ask him to sit again.

7. Repeat steps 5 and 6 until your dog is glued to the floor.

8. Now open the door a tiny bit.

9. Click and treat if he doesn't move out of position. If he does, just ask him to sit again.

10. Repeat steps 8 and 9 until he is reliably remaining in the sit stay.

Continue doing this, opening the door wider and wider, until you can have it completely open and your dog isn't moving a muscle. Then build to where you are outside of the door and your dog is still inside. For the second half of this exercise, you will need your dog to go through the doorway on your cue and immediately look back at you (rather than at any provoking stimuli).

11. Call your dog through the doorway and instantly say his name.

12. When he looks back at you, click and jackpot with tons of treats.

Once your dog is reliably waiting for you to call him through the doorway and looks back to you without you having to even prompt him to do so, it is time to practice this with every doorway you come to, every door in your house, car, crate—pick a door, any door.

You can also practice this when you come to any barrier or on sidewalks when crossing the street or a driveway.

BEHAVIOR NUMBER TEN: NO GUARDING OF OBJECTS, PEOPLE OR PLACES

Why You Need It

Many dogs aggressively guard objects such as toys, food, water, their crate, bones, furniture, their owner, clothes they have "stolen," or their "territory," such as the house, yard or car. Some dogs make guarding an art form and can even be possessive about certain spots on the floor or corners of rooms. "If I see it, it's mine," "If you have it, it's mine," "If you think it is yours, think again—it's mine" and "Even if I don't want it and you do, it's mine" mentality.

The adage that "It is better to give than to receive" needs to be taught to these dogs that don't like to share. It is much easier to teach a new puppy to share than it is to re-educate an adult that was *taught* to protect his resources; however, it isn't impossible to teach that older dog. It takes a great deal of patience, avoidance of punishment, and good management skills and a bunch of fun games in your training repertoire.

If your dog has a long history of and excels at guarding, you must be very careful when playing these games. You know your dog—watch carefully for warning signs or signs of stress and promptly end the game, even if he ends up "winning." I look at it this way: While it's true that he may have won this round, you get to live another day to work on the issue and don't have to spend time in the emergency room. And you'll know for next time to be careful not to push the session too long. Oops! Handler error! No big deal. Try again tomorrow.

Your mantra for these exercises is this: *"I will make it fun for my dog to drop stuff."*

> The ten foundation behaviors are bridge response, eye contact, name recognition, heel on a loose leash, accept touch, accept secondary reinforcers, stays, recall, control in and out of doorways, and not guarding objects, places or people. Whew! Sounds like a lot of training doesn't it? It is and it isn't.

No Guarding of Objects

How to Train It

The Two-Toy Game

This is a wonderful game that teaches the dog three very important things: (1) fetch, (2) come, (3) give (not to be possessive about objects).

This game has added benefits in that it builds relationships and gives the dog some aerobic exercise. The use of two toys is important because with two fun objects, you and the dog are not always engaging in a prey-ownership negotiation. If you do get into this kind of confrontation, you will lose no matter what, because even if you do succeed in getting the object out of your dog's mouth, you have now set the stage for guarding valuable resources.

1. Have two toys of equal value to the dog (identical toys work best).

2. Stand in the middle of the yard.

3. Throw one toy to the right, telling the dog to "get it."

4. When the dog gets the toy, encourage him to come to you. If you have to, wave the other toy you have. As he is on his way to you, say "come."

5. Tease him with your toy. When he drops his toy (not before—get the behavior, then give it a name), say "give" and then instantly throw your toy in the opposite direction, saying, "get it."

6. Repeat steps 4 and 5.

Be careful to end the game before the dog gets tired. In the beginning, throw the toys only a few times. Leave him wanting more! You will build desire, not only for the game, but for you as well. Do not take anything forcibly from your dog unless it will instantly kill him. If you do this, he may become reluctant to come close to you and stay far away, he may just run and hide after he steals something of yours, or he may bite you. If your dog has something in his mouth that you don't want him to have, trade him for it with something of equal or better value. If he has a tissue, offer him steak. If for some strange reason he prefers the tissue, let him have it—it won't kill him!

A few years ago I was working with a Golden Retriever that guarded objects from his owner. We tried playing the two-toy game. I gave him one toy. He promptly took off. I showed him my toy and made it wiggle and jump and be really interesting. He went off in a corner and wouldn't come near me. His attitude seemed to be, "Great. You have one, I have one— we're even." Alrighty then. I had the bigger brain—I had to use it. Ah ha! I grabbed five other toys off of the shelf. His eyes bugged out of his head ("Wow! Look at all the toys you have!!) in typical Golden fashion, and he raced to me and spit the one toy out of his mouth. After a few weeks of playing the six-toy game, we were able to go back to playing with two toys and he was longer reluctant to bring anything to his owner.

If your dog guards objects such as bones and won't even let you pass him while he is chewing on one, there are three things you can do to alleviate this problem. Which option you choose to do depends on your household, specifically, whether there are young kids around, whether someone in your family will not be compliant, how many other dogs you have, and how much time you can spend.

- You can let him have a bone, but put him in his crate, so you can walk safely around the house. This option is great when you have a multiple-dog household or if there are young kids running around. It doesn't teach the dog not to guard, but instead simply manages the behavior.

- You can throw him another bone or treats each and every time you pass him. You can also curve away from him, so that you aren't walking straight toward him. This way he may not feel threatened when you walk past. This exercise teaches him that you walking past is a good thing, not something to be afraid of, and is a great starter step for the "give."

- You can give him no bones to chew at all. In the beginning, depending on the severity of his guarding issues, this may be the safest option. That way, you can't make a mistake and he can't practice his guarding behavior if there is nothing to guard. Again, this doesn't teach the dog not to guard in the first place, but it is good management of the problem.

The Give-and-Take-It Game

This is very similar to the two-toy game, except you don't always throw the second toy. Just hold one toy out, and say "take it." Make your toy come alive and be more appealing than the one in his mouth. As he is dropping his toy, say "give," and then hold your toy out to him and say "take it." Do not pick up the one he dropped until he already has the second one in his mouth. Otherwise, you may still get into the "fighting over prey" behavior. Repeat billions of times.

You should also practice this game with inappropriate objects, such as razor blades, pens, tissues, paper, socks, shoes, underwear—whatever your dog normally "steals." Dogs know very well when you are upset because they have something dangerous. Your heart rate goes up, as does your temper. If you practice this game with the stuff you don't want him to steal, when he does grab your favorite shoe, he will readily give it up without as much as a tooth mark. You can also teach your dog to

> If your dog thinks "give" is a signal to race away, then by all means change your word. Popular alternate words are "drop" or "mine."

take inappropriate objects and bring them to you for a treat. Better that than having him eat a razor blade or your absolutely favorite shoes and end up at the emergency vet's office. If your dog is too nervous to drop the item, his teeth may chatter or vibrate, he may bare his teeth, growl, turn his head away or move away. Whatever you do, do not, I repeat do *not* lose your patience or reach out to his mouth to try to get the item. If he shows any signs of nervousness, just walk away and try again later. Be careful, be prudent, err on the side of caution.

It is not important that your dog drop the object into your hand. In fact, dropping it on the floor is better. When he does drop stuff, have a party—make it fun for him to spit out items he has.

I am playing the give-and-take-it game with Shadow. Photo by A. Kelly.

No Guarding of Food/Water Bowls

Why You Need It

Ideally, your dog needs to remain calm around food and actually welcome a human approaching his food bowl. In some cases a person approaching your dog is the trigger that may set off the guarding behaviors. Your dog may lift his lip, growl, snap, bite or freeze. In the case of food, your dog may begin to eat faster and may grumble while doing so. You don't want to get bitten if you accidentally drop a piece of food and go to pick it up. The concern is not simply that your dog may race over and gobble up a bit of dropped food, but that he may similarly divebomb dropped medication. Many human medicines are poisonous for dogs and you may to have rush to the vet. Brain damage, surgery, or even death can occur, even with the best of dogs that don't normally guard or protect what they perceive is theirs.

How to Train It

There are many different exercises you can use to teach your dog not to guard his food bowl. Starting with hand feeding his daily ration of food for specific behaviors is always a good idea. It is an easy way to equate "hands" with "food is coming." Never free feed (leave a bowl out with food twenty-four hours a day) these dogs—food is easier to guard when it is out all of the time, and you will miss out on a valuable and easy way to reinforce your dog. There is no law I know of that says you must feed your dog in a bowl. If at any time, your dog isn't comfortable, end the session. If your dog needs to do more repetitions than listed below to remain calm, then by all means, do more. Again, *be careful, be prudent, err on the side of caution.*

After a week or so of hand feeding, you can move on to these steps:

 1 Arm yourself with two bowls and a handful of food.

 2 Put one treat in each bowl, put one bowl on the floor and allow your dog to get it.

 3 As soon as he is done eating, take the empty bowl away and at the exact same time, hand him the second bowl. Repeat this step at least a dozen times. Once your dog is comfortable with this, you can move to step 4.

4 Now put a handful of treats into each bowl. Give him one bowl and before he is done eating, slide the second bowl filled with more treats under his nose, while you take the first bowl away. Repeat this step at least twelve to twenty times over the course of a few days. As long as your dog is okay with this, go on to step 5.

No guarding step 3: The dog is done eating, and you switch bowls. Photo by P. Dennison.

5 As your dog is eating, add more food to the bowl. Depending on your dog, in the beginning you may have to stand up straight and drop the food from your hand held high. Alternatively, you may be able to reach in so that he can see your hand approaching with more food and drop the food in.

No guarding step 4: The dog is still eating while you switch bowls. Photo by P. Dennison.

No guarding step 5: Adding food while your dog is still eating. Photo by P. Dennison.

6 You can also teach your dog to stay while you put the bowl on the floor. That way he won't race over to it until you release him. In the beginning, you may have to place your dog at a distance from the bowl or behind a sturdy barrier. You can even toss him some food as you are putting the bowl down, or have someone stand next your dog, reinforcing him for the stay.

No guarding step 6: The dog stays while the food bowl is put down. Photo by P. Dennison.

No Guarding of People and Territory

There are a few different ways guarding can manifest itself with you as the valued resource. Your dog may guard you from another dog, keeping all of your attention for himself. He may guard you from another person for much the same reason or because he may sense a conflict in the interactions between people—for instance, two people hugging can be perceived as scary to some dogs, and they may want to break it up before a fight ensues.

How to Train It

Other Dogs

Let's say your dog is guarding you from other dogs in the household. I used the following steps with my own dogs.

Teach all of your dogs a solid stay.

 Reinforce the guarding dog heavily for his stay while you pet another dog—you can even throw him treats, or just remind him to stay while you pet the other dog, and then go back and pet him. If he is really good at the stay and won't break it if you talk to him, you can also praise from a distance.

I am petting Beau, while at the same time I am tossing food to Shadow to reinforce his down stay. Photo by V. Wind.

 Play the "my name is" game—have all of your dogs lined up in front of you, with you as the tip of the triangle. Say each dog's name, give him a treat and then move on to the next dog. If at any time the guarding dog attempts to push the other dogs away, you should go in between and block him, set him up in the line again and start over. When doing this, be quiet—don't yell or say "no." Just insinuate your knee in between the dogs and he should get the hint to back off.

Family Members

I work with a married couple that owns a dog with just such issues. We think there was spousal abuse in Joey's previous home. He gets very nervous when Bob and Beth are close and has threatened Bob on numerous occasions. Joey also has a problem if Bob comes into certain rooms of the house when Beth is present. After only seven lessons, Bob and Beth can now hold hands and hug when Joey is in the room, and he is getting better about Bob entering a room.

How We Trained It

1. Beth and Bob approached each other slowly, while flinging wads of food at Joey.

2. Once Joey would watch them approach and lower his head in anticipation of treats, Beth and Bob stood next to each other, continuing to throw treats.

3. After a few repetitions, Joey continued to remain calm, so we added in Beth and Bob hugging, while food came raining down.

Couple hugging while throwing food on the ground for their dog. Photo by P. Dennison.

Couple walking while one person feeds the dog to keep her on the outside. Photo by P. Dennison.

4. They continued to do this for a few weeks, a few times per week.

5. Then we started to take a walk together. Joey instantly went in between Beth and Bob to split them up. He didn't react in any particular way, but I assumed he was still nervous about their closeness (yes, we erred on the side of caution) because of the position he took.

6. I had Beth and Bob walk so close to each other that Joey had no choice but to walk alongside Bob. Bob then fed him copiously as long as he stayed in that position.

7. Within minutes, Joey was content to stay on the outside of Beth and Bob.

We next worked on Joey remaining calm while Bob entered a room.

1. Beth had Joey on leash and was armed with tons of treats.

2. Bob announced that he was coming toward the room (which in the past set Joey off to attack), and Beth started to feed Joey *before he reacted.*

3. Bob stopped at the doorway—Joey was still calm—Bob retreated.

4. They repeated steps 2 and 3 numerous times, always having Bob retreat while Joey was still calm.

5. They then raised the criteria and had Bob take one step into the room, all the while reinforcing Joey for remaining calm.

As you can see, I broke down Joey's two main issues into tiny steps, so that there was almost no chance for him to aggress at Bob.

There are some instances where it only looks like your dog is guarding/protecting you, when in fact he is trying to protect himself. Someone may be approaching you and your dog head on, and your dog may perceive this as threatening—to him. Or your dog may only look like he is protecting the car or crate, but may actually be frightened of someone moving toward these enclosed areas and feel vulnerable, knowing he can't get away. So he postures, growls, bares his teeth and generally looks really scary in his attempt to keep himself safe. For further reading on guarding behaviors, see the recommended reading list in Appendix 2.

The key here is to make it fun for your dog to *not* guard anything. There are many dogs that were specifically bred to guard (each in its own niche). These include the Anatolian Shepherd Dog, Akbash Dog, Akita,

American Bulldog, Belgian Malinois, Belgian Tervuren, Bouvier des Flandres, Boxer, Briard, Bullmastiff, Caucasian Ovcharka, Dogue de Bordeaux, German Shepherd Dog, Giant Schnauzer, Great Pyrenees, Kuvasz, Leonberger, Lhasa Apso, Polish Lowland Sheepdog, Puli and Rottweiler. Of course, the key to making sure that these types of dogs are friendly toward people and will allow someone on your property is to get your dog from a reputable breeder who has stable temperaments in his lines, and then to heavily socialize the animal from puppyhood into adulthood. However, you must always understand that the propensity is still there. After all, our ancestors bred in these behaviors, not knowing at the time that we, in the twenty-first century, would find them potentially dangerous.

POINTS TO PONDER

❖ *A few minutes per session, a few times per day and you will start to see some progress. If you find the dog is improving and then all of a sudden is "forgetting," just go back a few steps and review.*

❖ *Be patient, be kind, be fun! Training should be as fun as play, because the behaviors needed are all just "tricks!" Training needn't be a chore—it is a great way to build your relationship and trust with your dog—and you will need these behaviors to work on the desensitization process.*

Enrich Your Dog's Mind:

Additional Behaviors To Teach Your Dog

Many of the behaviors listed below come from competition obedience, Rally obedience, sheepherding and agility. It doesn't matter if you have no interest in actually competing. The behaviors can all be used at one time or another to help keep your dog safe, focused on you and away from potential danger. They also help greatly during the desensitization process, because it is so important to keep your dog busy and not just sitting or standing still. There are actually a zillion useful behaviors you can teach your dog, but I am only touching on the most important "survival" ones to get you started. It really doesn't matter what you teach your dog to do, as long as the behaviors are incompatible with aggressing. The books listed in Appendix 2 discuss how to train many of these behaviors.

> He who has not first laid his foundations may be able with great ability to lay them afterwards, but they will be laid with trouble to the architect and danger to the building.
>
> —The Prince, Niccolo Machiavelli (1469–1527)

Ellen's rescued Beagle, Moni, had been biting her for a year. There had been times when Moni treed Ellen up on the counter and Ellen had to wait for her partner to come home so she could get down. Ellen was unable to pet Moni, put her leash on, pass her crate or even come into a room without Moni launching at her. She had scars all over from Moni's bites. She came to me to see if I could help her with this problem.

We taught Moni some simple cues—eye contact, name, come, sit, down, stay—and paired lots of food with Ellen's presence. We added in a light touch with wads of food and I had Ellen sing her favorite songs (to help her breathe) while interacting with Moni. Once Moni was comfortable with cues and food coming from Ellen (and Ellen comfortable with this as well), we put Ellen in charge of all of Moni's training. Then we added in specific behaviors to stop Moni in her tracks if she decided to attack Ellen.

To counteract Moni from charging Ellen, we taught Moni to do a drop on recall, directionals and "go to your mat." That way, if Moni was coming at Ellen, Ellen would be able to redirect her to an appropriate activity. Not only did Moni learn these behaviors quickly and happily, Ellen ended up only needing to use them a few times before Moni completely stopped aggressing at her.

A few months later, Ellen told me that Moni had started to aggress at her again. It turned out that Ellen's partner was getting angry with Moni for some of Moni's other issues, and was starting to be "not so nice" to her anymore. Apparently Moni became frustrated and redirected that frustration/aggression back onto Ellen due to the verbal punishment she was receiving from the partner. The instant we realized what was going on and changed the partner's behavior, Moni again stopped aggressing at Ellen. In addition, Moni also became much calmer around new people and dogs and has almost stopped harassing the cat.

OTHER USEFUL BEHAVIORS

Here are some further behaviors to train in addition to your foundation behaviors. It is important that you practice these behaviors before you actually need them and that you make them fun for your dog. Then, when you do need to draw on them, the behaviors will be in your muscle memory as well as your dog's. You won't panic, because you know what to do when faced with a scary situation and your dog won't panic because you are just playing "that game" again.

Crate Training

Crate training is an underrated and useful skill. Being comfortable in the crate is important for so many reasons, whether at home, the groomer's, a boarding kennel, or the veterinarian's for those planned or unplanned overnight stays. By having a crate in your vehicle, you avoid potential problems such as your dog crashing against the glass to get at people, dogs or bikes going by, or trying to eat the nice police officer who stopped you to tell you that one of your headlights is out. When visitors come to your house or any time you need to contain your dog to keep him and others safe, a crate is the way to go.

Automatic Sits with Continued Focus When You Stop Moving

With this behavior, if you need to stop, your dog won't continue walking without you. You drop your umbrella and need to stop to pick it up. Your dog keeps walking and oops! All of a sudden a person/dog comes from around the corner. If your dog knew to stop, sit and stay when you stopped moving, this would not become a problem.

Right and Left Turns

If danger appears, you can make a quick getaway in the safest direction for you. You are walking down the street and a person (with or without a dog) runs across the street directly at you. Doing a fast right or left turn will avoid an ugly scene.

About Turns

You can train your dog to turn 180 degrees to the right or left, again to make a quick getaway.

Stand for Exam (on ground or on table)

This is a must-have behavior for the vet's office.

Dog standing for exam on a table at the veterinarian's office. Photo by P. Dennison.

Shadow has dropped on command as he was running toward his provoking stimulus. Photo by P. Dennison.

Sit and Down Stay

In the later portion of your dog's recovery, these skills are great—they mean you don't have to retreat from danger at a run. There are times when retreating at a run is not feasible. As your dog becomes more comfortable with his provoking stimuli, you can just ask him to stay and reinforce him heavily.

Drop on Recall

Let's say your dog gets loose, runs across the road and you call him, not noticing in your panic that there was a truck coming. He is already on his way to you and you ask him to drop (lie down) and then stay; you then call again once the truck passes.

Drop as He Is Running Away from You

The collar slips off or the leash breaks and your dog charges after his provoking stimuli. You'll need him to drop on a dime.

Call Front

You are walking and all of a sudden a person and dog comes flying out of the brush. By calling your dog to front position, so he is looking at you and sitting, you can avert some dangers.

Instant Down

Your dog is fine with other dogs. You see a stranger's dog lunging and barking at your dog. Ask your dog to down and heavily reinforce him. You can even call him to front and then ask for a down. (Lying down and turning away may be perceived as an "I am not a threat" signal to the other dog.)

Dog and owner heeling.   *Oops, someone in sight, call front.*

Dog now in front focusing on his owner.

*Instant down.
Photos by P.
Dennison.*

Fast and Slow Pace

It is very important to practice these. If you see someone ahead who hopefully will be out of sight soon, you can move slowly. Conversely, if someone is coming up behind you quickly (for example, a bike or jogger) you can run and find an escape route.

Directionals

These are sheepherding behaviors, where the dog moves in the direction (right or left) you are pointing. This skill is very useful in getting the dog to move away from something scary and great for when you are running for the phone and your dog runs in front of you.

Shadow is moving in the direction that I am pointing. Photo by V. Wind.

Coming Away from the Other Dogs in Your Household

Teaching your dog this behavior will be especially useful if a canine tiff is about to start or is already in progress. This way, you don't have to get into the middle of the fray, possibly getting bit.

Lying Down Quietly around the House

This is a pretty obvious and very important skill.

Working Well for Others

This behavior is more for a long-term program for your human-aggressive dog. If your dog likes people, then by all means have other

My dog Shadow working for someone else. Photo by P. Dennison.

people train your dog from the beginning. It is important if you have a human-aggressive dog to pick one person who is willing to spend a little time at least two to three times per week with you and your dog to build up a relationship. Eventually—possibly even a full year later—that person should be able to work your dog (asking for simple things such as a sit, down, heeling, stays, come).

Accepting of Muzzle

You teach your dog to accept the muzzle *not* so you can use it during the desensitization process but so that you will have it as an option for the human-aggressive dog that may need to go to the vet before he is completely ready. This way, your dog is comfortable with the muzzle and will be less stressed, and you will be less nervous because you know he can't hurt the vet. Because you are less nervous, your dog also will be less nervous.

Shadow wearing his "face jewelry." Photo by A. Kelly.

Bridget is telling Shadow to "go visit."   *Shadow races up to Virginia and lies down. Photos by P. Dennison.*

"Go Visit"

Here, you teach your dog to go to the person you are pointing to and lie down, versus jumping and/or biting. For the human-aggressive dog, this is a more advanced behavior—not for the beginning stages of training.

Nose Target Your Hand

This is a great way to get your dog to look away from provoking stimuli without using a head halter or yanking him away. Make it a fun game and he will willingly look away in search of your hand. As an added bonus, you won't be arousing your dog or possibly putting him in a position where he may feel vulnerable, as you would be if you physically tried to make him look away.

Beau nose targeting my hand. Photo by J. Petersen.

Needy jumping through a hoop.
Photo by P. Dennison.

Get Off the Bed, Chair, Couch or You When Asked

These are simply just polite house manners!

BEHAVIORS JUST FOR FUN

These behaviors are not necessarily useful in day-to-day living but are important for the enrichment of your dog's mind, body and confidence.

- Retrieve objects
- Retrieve objects over a jump
- Jump through a hula hoop
- Moving stand (This one is great in a multiple dog household when you want to let one dog in or out and the other ones charge the door. You can just say "stay" and the other dogs will screech to a halt.)
- Learn hand signals for sit, down, and recall
- Spin to the right and left
- Weave in between your legs
- "Clean up"—put toys in basket on cue
- Roll over
- Settle
- Bow (I call it "ta-da" because bow sounds too similar to down.)
- Agility obstacles (tire, table, tunnel, weaves, teeter, A-frame, dog walk, chute, jumps)
- Ride a skateboard
- Balance on a board with a tennis ball nailed to the bottom
- Track (find the person whose scent "pad" he has sniffed or even just follow a scent of liver that you dragged)

- "Wipe your feet" (on a towel or mat)
- Wag tail on cue
- Close a door
- Ring a bell
- Pick out a sock with your scent on it from a pile of otherwise clean socks
- Find your keys
- Shake paw (a.k.a. "Nice to meet you!" This is great for dogs that are nervous about having their feet touched.)

Beau putting his toys away. Photo by A. Kelly.

Flute learning to ride a skateboard. Photo by P. Dennison.

Sadie learning to follow a scent of liver. Photo by P. Dennison.

Cody picking up my keys. Photo by A. Kelly.

The list goes on and on. Basically, any behavior you can think of—be it a clever trick or something silly—can be used to enrich your dog's quality of life.

It doesn't matter what you do, as long as you keep your dog's brain engaged in learning new things all of the time. Think about it this way: You get a new job and are learning all new skills. You are using your entire brain and come home each day tired and ready to conk out on the couch. After a few weeks or months, you become comfortable with the job and it is easier. You are now using only one half of your brain and come home and have the energy to take a mile jog. It is a year later and the job is a piece of cake and in fact, you are bored with it. You find you can write a letter to your friend, surf the internet, call around to find the best location for your next vacation, all while doing your job and now you are only using the tiniest bit of your brain. You come home raring to do something physical and start training for the marathon.

Giving your dog new things to learn and investigate and allowing him to utilize all of his senses in solving problems (up, under, around) will result in fewer behavioral problems and a dog more than willing to lie around on the couch at night.

INTERESTING DIVERSIONS

Consistent in All Contexts, a.k.a. How to Train Your Aggressive Dog to Ignore Distractions

Of course, your dog is perfect at home—it is when he is in the outside world that causes a problem. It is a Catch-22—you can't train your dog to be calm around distractions and provoking stimuli if he can't even see a dog or person without going berserk. Before you can start the desensitization process, your dog must be trained with the foundation behaviors given in Chapter Seven. So let's start with the environment alone, with no scary bad things around. Depending on where you live, finding safe places to train may be difficult. The most important thing to remember when selecting a few safe places to train is to not let your dog practice his aggression, so make darn sure there are no people or dogs around. Where there is a will, there is a way!

Because my background is competition obedience, I already knew the benefit of training in a myriad of different locations, so that my dogs could learn to generalize behaviors and be just as good at a trial as they were

FINDING LOCATIONS FOR TRAINING

❧ Call your local park's department. Tell them of your problem and ask if they have any newly acquired property tucked away in the area that no one goes to, or ask them if they know what hours the park generally is empty.

❧ Go to a dump or junkyard—few people or dogs hang out there. Be sure to put boots on your dog so he doesn't hurt his feet.

❧ Use tennis courts—these are generally fenced in.

❧ Go to schoolyards and parking lots in off-hours.

❧ Walk on a trail, *if and only if* you have someone with you to help who can look up and down the trail to warn you when someone is coming so you can veer off into the woods. This way you can be more relaxed and focused on your dog, and won't hyperventilate during the beginning of your training program.

❧ Call a local farmer and ask if you can use his fields to train your dog.

❧ Rent someone's training facility for an hour or so, making sure that no one else is coming in. Do not forget to lock the door.

❧ Go to your friend's backyard and train.

❧ Try your local businesses. Many large corporations have huge expanses of beautifully manicured lawns where you can go off hours.

❧ Visit dog parks or city parks or parking lots off hours.

during training. When I first started working with my rescued human-aggressive dog Shadow, I knew it had to be the same kind of thing—train in tons of places to be able to get the focus, attention and reliability before I started to work on the desensitization process. I had a few spots we could safely go for training and where he could just "be a dog." When working in public places, I would drive up and park and then walk around the entire site, looking for people and planning out escape routes, just in case someone surprised me. Once I deemed the site to be a safe one for Shadow (fewer than four people in an entire park), I took him out and trained him within two feet of the van, always being on the lookout for anyone coming. If I saw someone, I would whisk him back in his crate and wait until the person passed before I brought him out again. If there were too many people, I drove around and looked for another place to train that day.

As his foundation behaviors and attention to me improved, I worked him farther away from the van. Because I was always on guard and set up the training so there was a solid barrier (fence, lake, river,

*bushes) at my back, giving me one less direction to be worried about,
Shadow never practiced his aggression while we were training. I was also
lucky to be able to train off leash on a friend's sixty-five-acre farm a few
times per week.*

As mentioned earlier, you must train the ten foundation behaviors
(bridge response, eye contact, name recognition, heel on loose leash,
accept touch, accept secondary reinforcers, stays, recall, control in and out
of doorways and not being possessive) *before* working on the actual
desensitization process. It is imperative that your dog possess alternate and
incompatible behaviors that he knows like the back of his paw to draw
upon when provoking stimuli are present.

*At a recent seminar that I presented for aggressive dogs, the dogs were
so busy and intent on learning to ride a skateboard that I was able to get
within a few feet of them without them aggressing at me or my dog.*

REINFORCEMENT SCHEDULES

Part of being a good trainer is knowing how to use reinforcements
properly—not just using different types of things to reward your dog, but
actually understanding that it is important to know *when* to reinforce.

When teaching all of these behaviors, it is important not only to
break each one down into small pieces as you train them, but also to
know how to properly use reinforcements. As mentioned in Chapter
Seven, there are many ways to reinforce your dog other than the same
old one lousy cookie. There are three major mistakes people make with
food training:

1. They continue to use food as a lure or prompt. When used, food
   should be a reward, not a bribe (you can tell if you are bribing
   your dog if he won't do anything unless you have a treat in your
   hand) or a lure (luring should be used sparingly and only if the
   lure motion becomes the hand signal for the behavior). Otherwise
   the dog is only learning to follow your hand.

2. They fail to move into a variable reinforcement schedule once the
   dog has learned the behavior. Your dog will perform better if he
   doesn't receive food for every correct behavior. Be a slot machine,
   not a vending machine!

3. They don't work on the value of other types of reinforcers. You won't always have food with you. Build up the value of other types of reinforcements—petting, praise, play, sniffing.

The most obvious benefits of using other types of reinforcers is that you reduce the possibility of satiation to food and that you can train without having to always carry food with you.

People rarely get satiated with money as our main reinforcer because money is paired with almost anything that can be purchased, decreasing immensely the saturation point. Obviously, we can't make food as potent to our dogs as money is to us. However, we can also use life rewards paired with the clicker. Don't *compete* with the environment—*exploit* it! For example, if your dog is more interested in sniffing the ground than in paying attention to you, make a note to yourself that sniffing should be added to the list of things your dog finds reinforcing and then use it to your advantage.

Use the element of surprise when reinforcing—here is where your unpredictability comes into play. Even if delivering a treat, you can toss it up in the air, throw it ahead of you, or add funny noises while flinging it.

There are a few different schedules of reinforcement that you need to be aware of. Two of them are good and two you need to stay away from once a behavior is learned.

A **fixed interval** means you reinforce after the same amount of *time elapsed*—every five seconds, for example.

A **fixed ratio** means you reinforce after the same amounts of *behaviors*—for instance, after every third sit.

Both of these "fixed" schedules give rise to boredom, dullness, loss of focus, lethargy, a low performance rate and what is called "scalloping." Say your dog is heeling and, being the creatures of habit we humans are, we reinforce with a treat every fifth step. You will soon notice that as soon as you feed, your dog goes off in la-la land and then comes back to you after the fourth step to get his next "fix" of the treat. Is he being stupid or stubborn? Neither! *You* were being too predictable and boring.

When you first start out teaching a new behavior, a fixed ratio is fine. However, if you don't go to a variable ratio with reinforcement variety quickly, you can get what is called "scheduled induced aggression." For instance, suppose you pay out as though from a vending machine—every sit gets a treat, every down gets a treat. "Put a behavior in, get a treat." If you stay on the fixed schedule too long and then suddenly try to go to a variable schedule of reinforcement, you may create a dog that incessantly barks, whines, bites, and is generally obnoxious, or one that upon seeing that there is no cookie in your hand, will look at you and walk away. He is not defying you—you are just the broken vending machine. And why would he hang around, continuing to stick behaviors into a broken vending machine?

A **variable interval** means you reinforce after different amounts of time elapsed—after five seconds, twelve seconds, twenty seconds, three seconds, eight seconds, etc.

A **variable ratio** means you reinforce after different amounts of behaviors—for instance, after one sit, ten sits, three sits, nine sits, etc.

Both of these "variable" schedules create excitement, focus, desire, drive, intensity, animation and a high performance rate. And who wouldn't want that?

Perhaps you are doing an entire training session with sits, downs, eye contact, backups, etc. A slot machine would reward only a few of the behaviors in each sequence. Maybe out of ten sits, three are rewarded. You can also make the rewards more diverse (reinforcement variety). For example, for the first reward, you clap your hands and yell "yippee!" For the second reward, you run around and let the dog chase you and for the third reward, you feed fifteen treats. Your dog will work harder for fewer food reinforcements. Jackpot when he has performed a really spectacular behavior—for instance, when he has remained calm in a new and distracting place; started to run towards that prey object and when you called, came back to you; did a behavior that, for him, was really hard and the light bulb finally went on. Be creative and keep an eye on your dog. Keep in mind that even the most simple behaviors should occasionally be rewarded with a jackpot. For instance, if your dog is really wonderful about sitting on cue, don't take it for granted. Surprise him every now and then with a jackpot for that simple sit.

POINTS TO PONDER

❖ *There are quite a few behaviors that you can train to become part of your dog's behavioral repertoire.*

❖ *It is vital to train these behaviors before you work on the desensitization process. Trying to work around your dog's provoking stimuli without these behaviors intact is like putting a ten-year-old child behind the wheel of your car during rush hour traffic on the Cross Bronx Expressway and expecting him to make it home safely.*

❖ *Be creative when finding a safe place to train your aggressive dog.*

❖ *It is imperative to reinforce your dog correctly in order to create durable and strong behaviors.*

Designing Your Desensitization Program

So how do you begin to modify your dog's behavior? By using systematic desensitization, you can change your dog's reactions. As you know now, this is a slow but extremely effective process. The steps are minute, but if you follow them conscientiously, you'll achieve the desired results.

You now have your ten (plus one—I am a big fan of crate training) foundation behaviors in place at home and in some low distraction areas around town. To review, these are: bridge response; eye contact; name recognition; heel on loose leash; accept touch; accept secondary reinforcers; stays; recall; control in and out of doorways; not being possessive about objects, people or dogs; and crate training. You have also started to train the other behaviors in Chapter Eight. Now you are ready to use these tools to desensitize your aggressive dog.

RECORD KEEPING

Record keeping is very important in the desensitization process. It is too easy to forget where your dog is in his training for each kind of situation and then to make a mistake. Record keeping is also to your benefit—by looking back at your log, it gives you the opportunity to see your progress. If you are not seeing any advancement in your training, you can review and see if there is a pattern that you can then adjust. One such chart can be as simple as this:

Date:_____

Location:_____

Context: (describe in detail)_____

_____

Number of minutes:_____

Rate the behaviors practiced from 1-5, 5 being great:

__eye contact __name recognition __heeling on loose leash __recall __ sit

__down __stay __basic attention __door etiquette __crate training __accept touch

__other behaviors (describe)_____

Reinforcers used: _____

Any reaction? Describe in detail_____

You can then make a sheet for each context (circumstance) change. There are other sample charts in Appendix 1. You can also (and I know this seems a bit childish, but do it anyway) put a gold star on your calendar for each session in which your dog did not react. Put a red star for the sessions in which he did react. This is a very easy way to see any patterns (good or bad) that are starting and will help you know one of two things: (1) you are on the right track, or (2) you need to rethink your sessions.

GOAL SETTING

It is very important to have a short-term, mid-term and long-term goal for your dog. Because the process takes a great deal of time, having a goal keeps you on track and focused, and helps prevent you from giving up on your dog or yourself. Of course, it is important to make each goal attainable within the dog's ability at any given time.

The original goal I had for Shadow was to be able to compete in competition obedience, Rally and agility. As soon as I came to terms with his aggression, I dropped those ideas and just stayed "in the moment." However, once I started to see a light at the end of the tunnel and he began to act more like a "normal" dog, my goal was to start working toward his Canine Good Citizen test. I continued to train for those other dog sports, knowing that I might never be able to compete, but I wanted to enhance his life by teaching him new behaviors. When we accomplished his CGC, I moved on to Rally and agility and after four years of desensitization and training, we now compete safely and successfully.

Many of the dogs in my aggressive dog class are also "in training," some for their CGC, some for Rally or Freestyle—having these goals adds purpose, direction and fun to the long process of desensitization. Teaching their dogs the skills needed for these events also makes their owners darn good trainers!

CONTEXT DESIGN

When setting up your sessions, make sure you have willing and knowledgeable people to help you. If your dog is dog-aggressive, the other dog you pick to help you must be a neutral dog—one that will not react if your dog does aggress. Each context *must be completely controlled and orchestrated* and for this reason, you cannot use the general, unsuspecting, unknown and uncooperative populace. If your dog is aggressive/reactive to both dogs and people, do not use both to start—use people first (since you can't use a dog without a person).

In addition to setting up each context with compliant people/dogs, you must also plan your session out to the smallest detail. Exactly what will you be doing with your dog, what will your helpers do, what will you do if your dog pops off?

Let's take this one point at a time.

Exactly what will you be doing with your dog?

Draw on your foundation behaviors—that is what they are there for. Heeling, stays, recalls (don't drop the leash), sits and downs (you can make them fun—ask for a sit, then down, then sit, etc., all in rapid-fire speed), silly pet tricks—shake paw, roll over, settle, anything you have taught your dog to do.

A good desensitization session will include:

- Play
- Foundation behaviors
- Tactile factors (touching or petting)
- Learning something new (This can be anything you can think up or you can use the lists in Chapter Eight.)

When you play, be sure it isn't overly stimulating. Getting your dog excessively excited in the early stages of the process may end up backfiring. Heart rate goes up and excited behavior can quickly turn into a bite. If your dog gets extremely aroused when playing and doesn't know how to cool down quickly (yet), I would recommend avoiding toys in the beginning. If your dog does get aroused anyway, slow down and do something easy.

On the flip side, many dogs will not play in public if they are stressed. This is a nuisance because you cannot use it as a reinforcer, but it becomes a great barometer of your dog's stress level.

I was desensitizing a student's dog to the sound of someone knocking at the door. I was outside of my building knocking while his owner practiced recalls inside. Once the dog was consistently staying with his owner and not responding to me at all, I had his owner hold his collar while I came back in. Then, instead of continuing to train new behaviors, we all took a walk for fifteen minutes, just in case the dog was still feeling aroused. We did this so there was no chance of him redirecting any residual arousal to me. The moral? We did something hard (someone knocking on the door) and ended with something easy and fun (taking a leisurely walk in a field where there are great smells, being sure to pair positive associations with me—the scary person who had been knocking on the door).

Learning is inherently stressful, even using positive methods, so if you are working on something hard, be sure to end it with a nice quiet stroll.

You can also start your session with a nice walk and allow your dog to do what dogs do best—sniff. At my class for aggressive dogs, we always start each session with a long walk on the trail, at a far enough distance from each other so as not to cause distress for any of the dogs. After an hour on the trail, we then work on

Shadow having fun on the playground equipment, while Po is busy with her owner. At times we were within leash range of Po and she didn't bother aggressing at Shadow. Photo by E. Griffith.

each dog's issues. We have seen great strides in each dog's progress since we started opening the class with the walk. We are using positive associations to yield a better success rate, by pairing doggie heaven (great smells) with their provoking stimuli. After a short time—usually a few weeks of doing this—the dogs just settle down and rarely aggress at each other on the trail.

You will also need to plan out your reinforcers. In the beginning, depending on your dog's aggression level, using only food and gentle petting as reinforcers during a desensitization session may be the best thing for you. While you are training by yourself, by all means use a full range of reinforcers. Once your dog has a long history of calm experiences around his provoking stimuli, you can add play, games and toys as rewards for good behaviors.

"A long history" does not mean one or two or even three successful sessions. It means many *calm experiences—anywhere from ten to fifty or more* in each context, *depending on your dog.*

How long should the sessions last?

Your next decision should be how long the session should last. Anywhere from two to five minutes per session is more than enough to start with. Don't think your dog isn't learning anything even if your session is only thirty seconds—he is. He is learning not to aggress. You can do two to three sessions per day, with a minimum of an hour of rest in between. The key is always to end *before* he aggresses, not after. Quit while you are ahead! Remember, once your dog's adrenaline and glucocorticoid levels are raised, as well as all of the other hormones that are related to stress, you will have to wait for a few days for those levels to come down to normal. Any added pressure or anxiety will only spike those levels even higher.

While working with my aggressive dog Shadow, I make it a fun "challenge" for me to end the session before he shows any signs of feeling stressed.

What will your helpers do?

To start, the safest thing for them to do is simply to stand still. If your dog is human-aggressive, start with low density—one person, and if your dog is dog-aggressive, start with only one dog that you know will not react if your dog does. Make sure the handler of the neutral dog keeps the dog quiet—lying down is best. The distance should also be way beyond your dog's aggression threshold for a few reasons: you will be more relaxed and comfortable, your dog will be more relaxed and comfortable, and you can settle down and concentrate on practicing behaviors with your dog, continuing to build on the "muscle memory" of foundation behaviors. I have worked with dogs whose initial threshold was 500 yards away—gradually, over time, we were able to decrease that to inches away.

What will you do if your dog pops off?

Nothing. Really. As long as everyone is safe and far enough away (and they must be when you are starting out), you don't have to panic. Stand still, hang on tight, and lock your arms against your waist so the dog doesn't pull you off your feet or jerk your arm out of the socket, and so you don't inadvertently yank back.

Molly is reacting to Bo and Jim is standing still, holding the leash tight. At the same time, Lori is keeping Bo busy so he doesn't in turn react to Molly. Photo by P. Dennison.

Cody is trying to pull his way over to Belle. Pat is hanging on tight, locking her arms and not giving Cody more leash. Photo by P. Dennison.

As soon as your dog calms down or his body loosens up, call him to you softly, ask for a sit, down and one other behavior (anything will do), count to three and *then* calmly reinforce him for paying attention to you. If your dog reacts in any way or shows stress signs, then by all means move farther away (negative reinforcement—not the greatest option here, but that will just tell you that you goofed because you got too close). If you know your dog reacts at, say a distance of thirty feet, start at fifty to sixty feet away.

You want to be careful that you don't "boat the marlin." This means if your dog pulls or lunges, don't give him *more* leash and then try to reel him back in to you. Some people may think that since I am asking you not to yank back, it means you should just follow him if he pulls on ahead or let the leash out even more. If he hits the end of the leash, that's his problem—stand your ground.

If you find that your dog is aggressing within the two to five minutes, you need to stop and look back at your log sheet. Did the session go on too long, was his provoking stimulus too close, are your foundation behaviors up to snuff, did *you* lose focus or panic? Once you have identified the problem, it will be quite easy to fix. Your goal here must be zero reactivity from your dog.

If you have a hard time slowing down and are continually pushing your dog beyond his limits, think of this analogy:

You are driving in the snow on level ground. You come to the top of a big hill with a traffic light at the bottom. Where would you put on your brakes—at the top of the hill so you can navigate slowly and safely to the bottom, or would you wait until there was only a few feet between you and the traffic light before you jam on your brakes (most likely either hitting the car in front of you, ending up in a ditch or veering into the path of oncoming cars)?

STAYING FOCUSED

It is easy to lose focus when you are scared, nervous or unsure as to what your next step will be. To help alleviate this, be prepared before you take your dog out. If at the beginning you are hyperventilating, leave your dog

Being aware of your dog at all times while he is not safely secured is very important. After all, you don't want to have a great session, and then lose focus and have your dog aggress while going back to the house.

where he is for now. If having a one-minute session helps you remain calm, then by all means do it. If you lose focus or are unsure, your dog will pick up on this and will also lose his focus on you, which can lead to aggression. Be aware that each session starts the instant you touch the leash and ends only after the dog is safely secured (in house, crate or car) and that you must be constantly vigilant every second of every session.

SAMPLE SESSIONS

These next pages will take you through a few months of sessions. They are not to be followed just once for each stage—they are to be done over and over and over again, ad nauseam, until you are bored silly, before going onto the next step. Stick to no more than two to three sessions per day with an average of five minutes per session and at least thirty to sixty minutes between sessions. As you get further along in your training, you can gradually increase the length of your sessions to ten or even up to fifteen minutes. *You can insert a person or dog—whichever is your dog's hot button, into the following scenarios. For ease of reading, the provoking stimulus in these sessions is a person.*

Context One

Go to a quiet place and take your dog out of your car (using door etiquette). Let your dog sniff around a bit to get acclimated to the environment. Once he looks back to you and says, "Okay, why are we here?" you can have your provoking stimulus (for ease of reading, hereafter called "friend"), as far away as your dog needs her to be. Have her stand still or even sit in a chair and read a book. Set your timer for five minutes. Practice heeling—changing direction frequently to keep it fun—sits, downs, and recalls (from only a few feet away at first), teach him something new (pet tricks are excellent to do here), such as shake, wave, and bow, and then end the session. In Appendix 1, you will find a list of foundation behaviors, new behaviors and different types of reinforcers that you can copy and utilize to keep your sessions new, fresh and fun.

Take at least an hour break and do the same context—that is, with your friend sitting or standing—but change the order in which you practice the same behaviors.

Repeat this context for however many sessions it takes for your dog to remain calm at all times. Spread the sessions out over many days—three to four training sessions per week. Don't think you have to do all of this in one day. Ten one-minute sessions are better than one ten-minute session.

> Each time you change a context and add new criteria, you will need to make other parts of the session easier for your dog. In context two, your friend is now moving (new and harder criterion), so you want her to be farther away. Each time you add something new or harder in one aspect of your session, you have to lower other aspects of it (such as distance or duration). Doing this assures success.

Context Two

To change the scenario slightly, have your friend at a *farther* distance and ask her to walk slowly back and forth, not looking in your direction.

In the meantime, you will continue to keep your dog busy—heeling, come fronts, fast sits and downs, recalls, nose targeting your hand, etc. Again, keep the session to five minutes. Take at least an hour break and repeat, adding or subtracting some of the behaviors you are working on. Make sure you review foundation behaviors as well as adding in some new ones.

Two dogs and handlers far enough away so as to not cause a response from either dog. One person is "splitting" in between. Photo by V. Wind.

Context Three

Have your friend come a few feet closer, doing the same thing as on context two—walking back and forth slowly—while you continue to train your dog.

Context Four

Go to a different location and go back to context one.

Context Five

In location number two, repeat contexts one, two and three.

Context Six

Go to a third new location and go back to context one, then repeat two, and then three.

Context Seven

Go back to location number one and now have your friend a few feet

After a few short sessions, we were able to lessen the distance between both teams. One person continues to "split." Photo by V. Wind.

Here, we added a third person to the two people that the dog is already comfortable with. All people stay at a relatively far distance and are walking parallel. Photo by J. Petersen.

closer. If needed and your dog has another person that he already likes, have the "good" person walk in between your dog and your other friend.

Context Eight

Repeat context seven in all three locations, making sure the distance between your dog and provoking stimuli are always such that the dog can handle it and not aggress.

Context Nine

Once your dog can handle your friend at a close distance (say five feet), for at least ten separate sessions, add a second new person at a large enough distance so as not to evoke a response.

Repeat contexts one through eight with the new person.

Now that your dog can handle two people walking close to him, back and forth in the same direction in three different locations with no reaction whatsoever, go to context ten.

Context Ten

You now walk toward your friends, rather than having them walk parallel to you. Because this is a new context, widen the distance again between you and your friends. Watch your dog carefully and *before* he starts to get nervous, have your friends arc around you as you get closer. Repeat this, with the same far distance, in the same three locations.

Why am I suggesting that you practice in (at least) three different locations? Because dogs do not automatically generalize and what they learn in one location does not translate to all new locations. We learn to read at school and then know how to read on the bus, train, living room or anywhere we go. Dogs cannot apply their learning like this. To alleviate this problem, you must practice in many different places and build up to the same level of training in each one. By doing this, you will be better able to take your dog to new places and expand his horizons, all the while keeping his focus where it belongs—on you. After a time, you will see that he will be able to move to brand new places with ease and that he is fully generalizing.

Arcing or curving is seen by the dog as less threatening than walking directly at him. You can observe this yourself by watching two dogs approach—they will circle around each other and sniff hind ends, rather than head to head.

Satch the Bull Terrier and Beau the Border Collie are approaching head on and curve away from each other before Satch reacts. Photo by J. Petersen.

As long as your dog is doing well with the above contexts, move on to number eleven. If he isn't doing well and keeps reacting, then you are pushing the sessions. The more he practices aggressing, the better he will get at it, so make sure you keep the sessions well under his aggression threshold.

Context Eleven

Repeat all of the above contexts, using a third person. Be sure to introduce each person slowly and carefully, with many short sessions and pair the new person with the two people your dog is now comfortable with.

The above steps may take many months to achieve since you will be careful not to push the sessions beyond what your dog can handle. I did say that you would need to repeat these steps until you were bored silly, didn't I? If you try to rush the process, you risk having it take even longer, perhaps digging a deeper hole than the one you started with.

It took eight months of carefully planned sessions before Biscuit, a dog belonging to one of my students, would allow me to touch her for the first time.

Once you have three people that your dog can accept at a relatively close distance, you can now have them do something more than just walk slowly. People in the real world do not always walk at a snail's pace—they run, move erratically, scream (kids) and do all sorts of unpredictable things.

Context Twelve

Move your friends back again to a greater distance (back to thirty or fifty feet or more if necessary) and have one of them slowly jog parallel to you and your dog, while the other two simply walk slowly.

Context Thirteen

Have the jogger come a few feet closer.

Context Fourteen

Continue in this vein until the jogger can come fairly close without your dog reacting. Then the jogger can gradually increase her speed until she can go whizzing past and your dog is completely calm.

Greedy Trainer Syndrome— This is when the trainer gets greedy and wants more and more, faster and faster. When your dog is doing well, *don't* push him to get closer or have the session last longer. Quit while you are ahead! Trust me—you will be sorry if you push the session. If your dog aggresses during a session, ask yourself, "Was I greedy?" and mark it in your log.

Context Fifteen

Now have two of your friends go jogging past, but be sure to start at the far distance again.

Context Sixteen

Repeat contexts thirteen and fourteen until your two friends also are racing past and your dog is as cool as a cucumber. Don't forget, to reach this point, it may take five months or more, depending on your dog and how careful you are in setting him up to succeed.

Context Seventeen

Add the third person to the jogging group.

Not everyone in the world jogs in the same direction that you are walking; some people actually have the audacity to jog toward you, so you will need to train for this.

Context Eighteen

Starting at that far distance again, have one of your friends jog toward you. As she gets closer, you can arc away from her. Keep an eye on your dog and move slightly away before he gets nervous.

Context Nineteen

Have her come a few feet closer, while you continue to arc slightly away.

Context Twenty

Continue in this vein until the one jogger can come whizzing directly toward you and your dog remains completely calm as you arc slightly away.

Context Twenty-One

Add the second friend to the "jogging toward you" game. Once your dog remains calm with two people jogging toward him, go to context twenty-two.

Context Twenty-Two

Add the third person to the mix and again start from a large distance. Go through all of the steps listed above.

Context Twenty-Three

Go back to context twelve and have one jogger run erratically. Repeat contexts twelve through twenty-two with everyone running around and acting silly. Depending on your dog, you can have your friends wave their arms, again starting way back at context twelve, gradually getting closer and then adding more people.

Can you see the pattern here? Take one small step and repeat it many, many times, all the while making sure your dog is completely calm before going on to the next context change.

MORE FUN AND GAMES

There are two additional approaches you can add during the process. Once your dog is comfortable around a few people or dogs you can add in "grazing" and "protected contact." You can do these with any provoking stimuli—people or dogs.

Grazing

Context One

Have your dog and a neutral dog at a far distance from each other so as not to evoke a response. Toss wads of food on the ground and just let them eat. Repeat this a few times from a distance.

Context Two

Move a few feet closer and repeat—throw wads of food on the ground and just let them eat.

Context Three and More

Keep going closer and closer, while spreading the food out like grass seed.

Caveat: if your dog guards food, do not do these contexts at a close distance and be sure that your dog is out of leash range of the other dog. Work the guarding behavior as a separate session.

Two neutral dogs and one reactive dog all chowing down and completely calm. Photo by J. Petersen.

Why would we want to do this in the first place? Head down and sniffing can be calming signals and while we can't "make" our dogs do this, we can try to replicate it by giving them something to sniff around for. For some dogs, this takes the stress out of the process (for even with the best intentions, sometimes your dog may be stressed). When they see other dogs chowing down, it helps them relax.

I have done this with many dogs, most notably Satch, a dog-aggressive dog. Within a few sessions he was approaching the neutral dogs, quite content to sniff and snort around and find treats. He became so calm due to this and other exercises that he can actually now sniff the other dogs, allow them to approach head on and do a down stay while dogs are flying all around him. He is now ready try for his Canine Good Citizen certificate!

Bear, on the opposite side of the fence, is food-aggressive with other dogs. With the use of protected contact, we were able to easily and safely have two dogs in close proximity while feeding. Photo by V. Wind.

Protected Contact

Depending on how far along your dog is in his training, protected contact is a great way to proceed with the desensitization process. Protected contact is just that—completely secure fencing that separates the dog and the scary bad thing, keeping both parties "protected." Tennis courts, batting cages, and backyard fences are all great for this kind of context. Protected contact is not about pushing the dog beyond his limits—it is about bringing the training to a new level, in a safe, nonthreatening way, at all times setting your dog up for success.

Why should I use protected contact?

Many reasons! Protected contact is safe, and the dog is not feeling threatened or restrained by the leash. There is no risk if the leash breaks or is ripped out of your hand. In addition, it is a fantastic way to be able to ignore outbursts from your dog—you don't have to respond in any way, and your helpers don't have to jump back in fear of getting bitten. The added bonus is since you know everyone is out of danger, it is easier for you to remain calm.

Murray is too busy going through a tunnel to be worried about the group of us outside of the fence. Photo by P. Dennison.

When should I use protected contact?

There are two situations where you can use protected contact:

- ❧ Protected contact can be used after an extensive training history, with a long record of calm behaviors in many situations. Let's say you have a dog-aggressive dog that is doing fabulously around other dogs, but you are still nervous about direct, within-leash-range contact. Or perhaps you are nervous about having people approach, pet and feed your human-aggressive dog.
- ❧ Protected contact can also be used in the beginning of the desensitization process if you are so nervous or scared that your fear will affect your dog's behavior.

When I first started the actual desensitization process with my dog Shadow, I was petrified beyond belief of his aggression and there was no way I was going to let anyone near him without a solid barrier in between—even knowing he was on a leash didn't help me remain calm. I used protected contact from the very beginning and for many months after that.

Are there times I should not use protected contact?

There are some dogs that I would feel uncomfortable doing protected contact with from the onset—dogs that have no training to start and no relationship, connection or bonding if you will, with their owners. Name recognition and recall are a must before allowing them off leash—even within a fenced-in area. If your dog is still reactive toward the scary bad thing even at a distance and there are no foundation behaviors intact, he will just have more opportunity to charge the fence. If you have to rely on the leash to control your dog, then your dog is not ready for protected contact.

How do I use protected contact?

Once you decide that your dog is ready to use protected contact, set up your contexts much in the same way that you have done before. You and your dog are on one side of the fence doing all sorts of behaviors and you may drop the leash or take it off entirely. The other person or dog is on the other side of the fence. This may be the first time your dog has been off leash around his provoking stimulus, so make sure your helpers are at a far distance to start. As

Ellen and Moni are inside the fence, Ethel outside the fence. One of Moni's issues is moving feet. Here, Ellen throws food on the ground while Ethel walks in place. Photo by P. Dennison.

Richard and Pepper are inside the fence, I am outside the fence. Pepper is aggressive toward people, especially ones leaning over. Richard is feeding Pepper so her head is turned away. Photo by J. Zimmer.

with all of the contexts we have discussed, set your dog up to succeed. If you are working at a distance of fifty feet, don't suddenly jump to five feet.

You can play the "grazing" game; practice recalls, heeling, sits, downs, stays; play, anything you want to keep your dog focused on you. If your dog races to the fence to look at your helper but is quiet, stay calm, and call him back to you in a soft happy voice and heavily reinforce him when he comes to you.

Huck has a problem with people who lean over and reach their hands out to pet him. This is the distance I began at in our sessions, in reaching down as if to pet Huck. Photo by V. Wind.

Two days later, Florence and Huck are inside the fence, I am outside. Huck is completely unconcerned and in fact, has started to take the "cue" of people reaching toward him as a cue to look at Florence. Photo by J. Zimmer.

Eleanore and Jake are inside the fence. I am outside the fence with Beau. Jake is aggressive toward other dogs and yet is coming to Eleanore when she calls him, not giving Beau a second glance. Photo by J. Zimmer.

Cody (neutral dog) is busy eating food on the ground. Because he is not doing anything threatening, Austin feels comfortable in approaching him without aggressing. Photo by V. Wind.

Po is reacting to Needy who is outside of the fence. Because everyone is safe, Anna feels comfortable in walking away from Po. Photo by P. Dennison.

Po relaxes her stance. Photo by P. Dennison.

Po decides that Anna is more fun and stays with her. Photo by P. Dennison.

If your dog races to the fence and aggresses, stay calm and don't say anything. Make sure your helpers do not move away at all. Otherwise they would be *reinforcing* his behavior—the aggression worked in driving them away. Just wait for his body to relax and then call him to you in a soft voice. Once he gets to you, have him do three behaviors (such as sit, shake and down) count to three and *then* heavily reinforce. If you try to call him when he is supercharged and aroused, you are wasting your breath—he literally can't hear you.

As mentioned earlier, if you reinforce the instant your dog comes back to you in this case, you will see an increase of aggression. He will learn this really cool behavior pattern of "aggress and then

You may think your dog has selective deafness when he is ignoring you when aggressing or aroused, but he literally cannot hear you when in this state. A study conducted in the 1960s fitted a cat with an electrode, which was hooked up to a special device able to show when the cat heard a sound. A few mice were brought out and kept out of the cat's reach, causing frustration and tension to the cat. When a tone sounded, the machine registered that the cat's auditory nerves *did not record hearing the sound.*
We humans go through this same phenomenon when we are so engrossed in something stressful or tension-producing that we literally do not hear the people around us. This is our bodies' way of protecting us from an excessive load of stressful information.

come back for a treat." You must put some time in between the aggressing and the reward, which is why I recommend the three behaviors plus three seconds. Then he will make the correct association with exactly what he is being reinforced for.

THE ACTUAL APPROACH

Many times, you may be able, with enough time and patience, to desensitize your dog enough so that he ignores people or dogs in the immediate vicinity. There may come a time that you want more—you want direct contact. Before you decide that you want more, ask yourself this one question: Is direct contact really that important? Other than your veterinarian and a friend or two or boarding kennel, it really isn't essential that your dog have direct contact with other people and he can live a full and enriched life without it. However, if you feel you do need to train direct contact, do so under the following guidelines.

Caveat: Unless your dog has a *long* history of calm behaviors under his belt, do not even attempt direct contact.

There are two different ways you can do this: (1) you can let your dog approach your helper, or (2) you can have your helper approach your dog.

Option one is easier to start with and less threatening to your dog. Be sure you practice recalls constantly, with lots of reinforcement (jackpots); in case your dog gets nervous, you will be able to call him back instantly. Once your dog is comfortable approaching people, you may think that going to option two won't be a problem. Don't assume! This is very different and may be difficult for your dog to handle, so be sure to keep the session to one or two "seconds" and then call your dog back and have your helper leave at the same time. If you are the slightest bit nervous, by all means use protected contact in the initial stages.

To Feed or Not to Feed

When working with a human-aggressive dog, there will come a time that your dog is just becoming comfortable near one, two or three people. Many people will then want the helper to start feeding your dog. I understand the theory behind having the helper feed the dog—classical conditioning going on—people equals food, versus people equals fear. However, until the dog is exhibiting calm behaviors in many sessions with close proximity to people with no outbursts, it is better to have the dog's owner deliver the food rather than your helpers. That way positive association learning can still take place, but you avoid the risk of unexpected aggression.

If your dog willingly and nicely approaches one of your helpers, *you* praise and feed him. Why? Because hands coming toward a dog's face can be perceived as threatening, even when they carry a peace offering. Many dogs may aggress before or even after taking the treat. There is a funny gray area where a dog may develop the drive to approach people in expectation of something pleasant, but then get freaked out and aggress if the person moves. You have to be sure your dog is rock solid in all the above contexts—people, people in close proximity, people with movement—before you start having the helpers deliver treats.

After many repetitions of your dog approaching (and you can do this with protected contact) calmly and you feeding, you can then have your helper drop food on the ground or better yet, toss the food behind the dog so he has to turn away to get it.

Adding Touch

As with adding food, go slowly. When having a helper touch a human-aggressive dog, do this in a few, very specific steps:

❧ Have your friend reach out both hands simultaneously—one to feed a wad of treats and one to lightly touch the side of the neck or chest. It is very important that her hand approaches from below the dog's head. She must avoid leaning over or touching the top of his head or withers area. From the dog's point of view, these may seem very threatening, especially from a stranger. The helper must not touch him first and then feed, but feed and touch at the exact same time. She should be careful not to get into a full petting routine—this may be too scary—just one gentle touch, perhaps on the side of the head or neck. She should avoid a touch on the top of his head and avoid direct eye contact. She can turn her head away and even yawn or lick her lips (using some of the signs that dog use among themselves).

❧ The instant the dog is done eating, the touching hand goes away.

❧ Repeat only once or twice in a session during the beginning stages. You must watch your dog carefully for any signs of nervousness and stop the session before he aggresses.

❧ As each session progresses and your dog continues to remain calm, your helper may reach out a hand first to touch him and, within a half second after touching, then feed him. As soon as he is done eating, the touching hand is removed.

So at step four, your helper is now touching your dog first and then feeding. Gradually lengthen the time of the touch, but at this stage of the game, always end with a treat.

POINTS TO PONDER

❧ *Learn to read your dog and heed his stress signals. It will help immeasurably if your helpers are also well versed in your dog's body language.*

❧ *Set short-term, mid-term and long-term goals, making sure they are attainable and not pipe dreams.*

❧ *Plan out your sessions to the smallest detail (distance, duration, activities, reinforcers) in advance. Have a backup plan in case your dog hasn't read what you had planned and he decides that he isn't up to that context today.*

❧ *Stay focused and calm at all times. If you are doing this correctly, your dog can't hurt anyone because they are far enough away or behind a barrier.*

❧ *Keep a log. Oh so boring, and oh so important! You'll be able to go back and see progress. You'll also be able to see any trends one way or another, so you can either rejoice or change what you are doing. The entries don't have to be fancy—just a few words or sentences can suffice. If you can, videotape your sessions once a month, date them and keep them on file.*

 # Life with Dog

No matter what issue your dog has, or what breed of dog he is, the "recipe" for the systematic desensitization process is exactly the same. As you have seen, the key to training any behavior (including not aggressing) is to know how to break each one down into the tiniest of approximations (steps) and then train each step.

In the last chapter, a few broad problems were discussed and broken down; getting closer to your dog's provoking stimulus, whether it be a dog or person, being comfortable with movement coming from different directions, and the proper use of protected contact.

THE REAL WORLD

I do understand that "life with dog" is real life. We don't live in a vacuum and neither do our dogs. In the beginning, however, each and every context *must* be controlled *100 percent* of the time. But there will come a time that you will need to branch out and expand your dog's experiences.

Don't even attempt any of these contexts unless you have the prerequisite foundation behaviors—you will be setting your dog up to fail, allowing him to practice aggression, and making the aggressive behaviors just that much more ingrained. Every aggressive act is like a $100.00 withdrawal, and every positive experience is like a $1.00 deposit. Make sure you have at least 100,001 times more positive than negative experiences. This should be the yardstick that governs how you set up your contexts and training sessions.

I think the mistake that most people make is that they assume that they have a right to go anywhere with their dog at any time. This is not true. You have to train your dog before you can go for walks, and then train some more before you go for walks in very stimulating places, like on a trail. If your dog aggresses with people around, you simply cannot (yet) go for walks when people are around, period.

Let's talk about setting up your sessions to work on specific issues or just living with your dog while incorporating foundation behaviors.

Context—Walking on a Trail

Foundation Behaviors Needed

- *Walking on a loose lead*
- *Heeling with attention*
- *Sit*
- *Down*
- *Stay*
- *Name response*
- *Come*
- *Eye contact*

You are walking on a trail that usually doesn't have too much traffic. You are letting your dog just be a dog (on a long leash), sniff around and explore. You see someone walking toward you and you call your dog to you. There are a few options you can pursue depending on where you are in your training:

- You can ask him to heel with attention and continue on. Make sure you are between the person approaching you and your dog—this is called "splitting" and will help keep your dog calm. Feed the heck out of him as you pass.
- You can pull off to the side of the trail (the distance depends on your dog's reactivity at this point—make sure you pull off far away enough to keep your dog under his aggression threshold) and utilize a sit or down and stay. While your dog is in a stay, you can broadcast food all over the ground to keep him busy sniffing and eating.

❖ You can just turn around and hightail it back to your car, making it a fun game to run away from a stranger.

I was at an outdoor match show with Shadow, at an early stage of his training. I was off to one side, minding my own business, but constantly scanning the environment. I saw this young girl look at us with that expression that puts fear in the hearts of owners with human-aggressive dogs. Her eyes were saying, "I love dogs and I will pet your dog." I started to run back to my van and the girl sped up to catch us! We ran even faster and so did she. I was within three feet of getting him back to the van safely, but the girl

Jeff and Carole leaving the trail with Ebony as two fisherman walk past. Photo by P. Dennison.

Virginia with Needy and me with Shadow, continuing on the trail while the pedestrian walks by. We are between our dogs and the stranger (splitting). Photo by L. Weisner.

Virginia with Needy and me with Shadow, parallel walking on the trail. Both dogs are afraid of people. Photo by L. Weisner.

was faster than me. Shadow whirled around and aggressed at her. She backed off and I put him away. I realized that I needed to work on that specific thing—people chasing us, so I didn't get caught again. I made it a fun game for Shadow to have seven people chase us around. As an added bonus, I had them run up to us with arms outstretched, saying, "Can I pet your dog?"

If you absolutely must walk your dog on a street, then map out your course ahead of time and plan out your escape routes. Know the schedules of your neighbors and, if possible, enlist their help in letting you know when they or their dogs will be outside.

Context—Getting Safely into the Vet's Office

Foundation Behaviors Needed

* *Eye contact*
* *Name response*
* *Door etiquette*
* *Stay*
* *Sit or down*
* *A few pet tricks*

Since you have been practicing working on control going in and out of doorways, getting into the office should be pretty easy. Be sure to go in first without your dog so you can see where the problem areas may be. Once you have gotten into the waiting room safely, sit in a far corner and ask your dog to do a down stay and feed the heck out of him. If you think your wait might be long, you have two options:

* You can take him outside and ask the receptionist to let you know when the vet is ready for you.

* You can work on eye contact, sits and downs in rapid succession (called "puppy pushups"), hand targeting, settle, rollover, bow, shake paw, spin in a circle—all of these to keep your dog busy. Be sure to keep an eye out for people who become too interested in coming close to your dog and tell them in a nice but firm manner to stay away. You can always say your dog is afraid of

people (or dogs) and most people will honor that and not try to approach. You can always lie and say your dog has the communicable form of mange.

You should do many "dry runs" to the vet's office during slow business hours before you even need to see the vet. Go in, sit down, keep your dog busy for a few seconds, heavily reward for calm behaviors, and then leave. Repeat lots of times until you and your dog are comfortable.

When I took Shadow to the vet for the first time, I talked to the vet and technicians ahead of time and gave them the entire rundown of Shadow's issues. I told the vet that if Shadow did react, to please "freeze" and let me handle it. I actually threatened him (nicely), saying that if he ruined all of my training, heads would roll. I was lucky—this vet was very good with Shadow and Shadow fell in love with him instantly.

The moral of that story? Protect your dog from harm from well-meaning but unknowledgeable people.

Context—Having Someone Touch Your Dog in More Intimate Ways (such as a stand for exam for competition, measuring for his height card for agility or a vet exam)

Foundation Behaviors Needed

* *Eye contact*
* *Name response*
* *Stay*
* *Sit, down or stand*

Observational Skills You Will Need

Know what your dog's signs of stress are. If he gets too nervous, end the session *before* a growl or bite happens. Keep these sessions to just one to three repetitions before moving onto something different.

Let's say you have worked on getting your dog to accept some light touches from your helpers and want to take this a step further. You need to do some prep work for this yourself before adding other people.

1 Place your hand on the top of your dog's head and wait for him to look at you. Once he does, click and treat.

2. Repeat until a touch on the head causes him to stare at you adoringly.

3. Do this with a light touch on every body part—head, withers, feet, back and tail.

Once you add some helpers, you will utilize your stand and stay cues and while standing right in front of your dog, you will:

4. Shovel food in his mouth while your helpers walk up to him, around him and then walk away. The food stops when they walk away.

5. Repeat a bunch of times until your dog is comfortable with this.

6. Now gradually fade out most of the food and make "a person approaching" a cue for the dog to lock eyes with you and just feed him when he is looking at you.

Once he is comfortable with that aspect, you can add in the touching portion. Go back to shoveling food while your helper touches in ways typical for a vet exam or measuring. Start with just one kind of touch, for instance, touching the top of his head or withers or running your hand along from head to tail. At any time, you can remind him to "stay," and continue to feed. You will see your dog relax and focus on you for longer periods of time, so that now "a person approaching and touching" has become a cue to stay and look at you. Gradually you will add in longer and more obnoxious petting and handling on different parts of his body, depending on the needs of your dog.

When I needed to have Shadow measured for his height card in agility, I also added me holding his collar in a death grip into the desensitization process. This way, if either one of us was afraid during the measuring and I held tightly to his collar, he wouldn't be nervous. Shadow handled it like a trooper and was completely calm.

A complete stranger touching Shadow. His eyes are locked on mine. Photo by V. Wind.

Context—Guests Coming to the Door

Foundation Behaviors Needed

- *Crate training*
- *Verbal cue, "go to crate" or "kennel up"*
- *Crate door etiquette*
- *Come*
- *Name response*
- *Down stay*

Let's break the unwanted behavior sequence down. Right now, the cue is the doorbell, the behavior is storming the door in total arousal and the consequence may be that he gets yelled at (positive punishment—something added that he doesn't like to decrease behavior—oops!), consoled (positive reinforcement—something added that he likes to increase behavior—oops!), or dragged away (negative reinforcement—something taken away that he didn't like to increase behavior—oops!). If you let him stick around while guests are instructed not to interact with him, he may still be too aroused and may react badly.

You now need to change his behavior and consequence as it relates to the cue. The cue is still the same—the doorbell. Rather than have him think the doorbell is a cue to aggress, teach him that the doorbell is a cue to go to his crate. Then once the guests are in and all sitting down, you can (depending on the level of training) go and get him (on leash), heavily reinforce him for focusing on you and for calm behaviors around guests.

1. Arm yourself with tons of treats and a willing friend. Have your friend ring the doorbell. Call your dog to you and run with him to the crate, saying your "kennel up" cue word. Give him wads of treats for getting in the crate. Keep the crate relatively close to you to make it easier for the dog. Release him from the crate and do it again—the doorbell rings, you and your dog race to see who can get to the crate faster, tons of treats happen in the crate, start a new repetition. Repeat this about ten times. Usually by that time, your dog is starting to figure out that the cue is the doorbell, the behavior is "get in my crate" and the consequence is that he gets wads of treats.

2. In a different session, repeat step one once to review, and then on the second rep, just stand there once the doorbell rings and wait. Let's see if the dog can figure this out by himself, without you running to the crate with him. Wait for at least fifteen to thirty seconds. If he doesn't run to the crate, help him a little by looking toward the crate and whispering "kennel up." Once he is in the crate, give him wads of treats. Repeat again and help him as little as possible. Do about five or six more reps, continuing to have a party each time he gets in his crate. Most dogs will "get it" by this time, but if yours doesn't, don't worry—just keep trying.

3. Now you want to increase the time he is in his crate before you give him treats since you really don't want to have to run to the crate (depending on where the crate is in your house in relation to the door) each time the doorbell rings. Your bell ringer rings the bell, the dog goes to his crate and you walk slowly to the crate while he waits patiently for the party. Keep doing this, gradually increasing the time he stays in his crate before feeding him.

4. It is time to add real live people into the mix. Start this with one person, not fifty. The friend rings the bell, your dog races to his crate, and you mosey on over to the crate and lock the door. Let

the person in the house and have him or her sit quietly while you race to the crate and have a party with your dog.

5. Do not rush to get to this step. It will take as long as it takes or you may never be able to have your dog loose in the house while guests are over. It is preferred that you use people with whom your dog is already comfortable for this step. Follow step 4 but after the party with your dog, bring him out of the crate (on leash) using crate door etiquette and heavily reinforce him for paying attention to you. Stay out of leash range! Practice down stays as well as eye contact, and a few pet tricks while you all sit around and chat. Keep the sessions short—literally a few seconds at first and stop before he gets stressed. Repeat a bazillion times. If he becomes wild and frenzied, you have pushed him too fast. Say nothing, do nothing (other than hang on tight to his leash—don't yank back) and wait for him to chill out. Most certainly move away (negative reinforcement—oops!) if he is within leash range (if he is—handler error, do not pass go, go straight to jail) to keep every one safe. Reinforce him after at least ten seconds for the calm behavior and try again in a few minutes. Repeat the process again until he can remain calm at all times—from the ringing of the doorbell, to his racing to his crate, to you allowing your guest in the house, to you having a party in the crate, to putting the leash on, to bringing him in the room where your friend is.

Once he remains calm with each of these steps, you can gradually add one additional person at a time. Be sure you use people that your dog is already comfortable with.

Steps one through four may seem like they would take forever; in reality, most dogs figure it out in a day or two of diligent practice.

Context—People or Dogs Walking Past Your Window or Yard
Foundation Behaviors Needed

- *Eye contact*
- *Name response*
- *Come response*
- *Stay*
- *Some pet tricks, including hide-n-seek*

Windows: The best thing for this kind of reactivity is management; block the windows with curtains or some such sight barrier. If for some reason you really can't block the view, you can teach your dog to remain calm about the world going by. Set up the situation and have friends help you by walking past your property, continuing back and forth until they hear your dog being quiet. If your dog is reacting and they totally move away, then they are reinforcing your dog for reacting. Your job inside the house is to keep your dog focused on you. Practice doing stays, any kind of pet trick and periodically run out of the room and hide and then call the dog to you. Have a big party once he finds you. In essence, you want to make it fun for him to move away from the window. You can even go up to the window with him and say something silly like, "Oh, that's just Auntie Mary," and just walk away. On the rare occasions I actually have my drapes open, I have done this with cats going past my windows and my dogs stop barking and come with me as I leave the window.

In the yard: Essentially you are doing the same thing. Go outside with him and keep him busy while your friends go back and forth. They can be walking, jogging, riding bikes and walking neutral dogs. (One context at a time, please.) Be sure you don't have them walk right next to your property at first—do this from a distance to start with. If you have a fenced-in yard, don't let your dog go outside unless you are with him.

Context—Driving in the Car (stopping for gas, going through a toll booth or drive-up window)

Foundation Behaviors Needed

❖ *Crate training*

❖ *Stay*

❖ *Eye contact*

❖ *Hand targeting*

There are really a few additional things you need to do to make this a successful event:

❖ Have a second person with you or very fast legs as you race around the car once you have stopped so you can feed the dog.

❖ Have the dog crated or at the very least behind some sort of barrier or in a seat belt. If he is in a crate, you can cover it with a lightweight sheet to block his view. You *cannot* allow your dog to be loose in the car. Flinging himself at the windows, teeth bared and snarling will do nothing to help him or your confidence and certainly will make passing money through the window quite dangerous.

Depending on your dog, avoid having him with you when getting gas if you don't have someone to help you, especially in the beginning of the retraining process. You can start desensitizing him to people approaching the car even before you put him in these actual situations. Have one of the helpers that your dog likes walk up to your car and fiddle with the gas cap while you feed your dog for calm behavior. Repeat bunches of times until he no longer reacts. If he does react, make sure your helper doesn't leave until he calms down.

Once you are ready to do the real thing, as you pull up to the gas pump, window or toll booth, have your helper feed the heck out of your dog (not just one or two treats—I am talking handfuls of treats, his entire daily ration of food if necessary) *before* he reacts. If he does react, the food stops. If he reacts and won't calm down, try not to leave the gas pump until he is calm or ask the attendant to stick around (maybe enlist his help ahead of time) until your dog is quiet (otherwise you will be negatively reinforcing him—oops!).

If you have no choice but to go it alone, here are some ideas:

❖ Toll booth—If there is no one behind you, stay put until he calms down.

❖ Drive-up window—This situation is easily avoidable, so don't put yourself in it unless you can readily reach back to feed your dog for quiet behavior.

❖ Gas—Get out of the car and race around to wherever the crate is and shovel food for quiet behavior.

You can also keep him busy doing behaviors even while in the crate, such as down, sit, nose target your hand, stay.

Key phrases to use so you won't have to come out and tell people your dog is aggressive, but they will still stay away— No doubt you have experienced it: You are minding your own business and keeping your distance and the general populace encroaches on your dog's threshold. Now, since you are watching your environment more carefully, you can see these people or loose dogs coming from a far distance. Try these phrases:

- "Stay away! My dog has been sprayed by a skunk!"
- "Stay away! My dog has a communicable disease!" (you can make something up beforehand)
- "Stay away! My dog is in training!" (you can get one of those bright orange "dog in training" vests)
- "Stay away! My dog is afraid of..." (whatever it is that is coming toward you)

For a loose dog problem, you can throw tons of food at the offending dog and then hightail it outta there, all the while yelling at the top of your lungs, "Come and get your dog *now*! My dog...

- "...has been sprayed by a skunk!"
- "...has a communicable disease!"
- "...is in training!"
- "...doesn't like other dogs!" or "...is afraid of other dogs!"

A BUSY DOG IS A HAPPY DOG

As you can see, with careful planning you *can* do regular activities with your aggressive dog if you break the issues down and incorporate foundation and new behaviors within those activities. Rather than doing the often recommended, "put the dog in a down stay while provoking stimuli are around," the better bet is to keep him busy. By having just one behavior (such as the static stay) in your dog's repertoire, you are limiting his ability to cope. A busy dog is a happy dog.

As Dale Carnegie says in his book, *How to Stop Worrying and Start Living*, "It is difficult to worry while you are busy doing something that requires planning and thinking," and "The remedy for worrying is to get completely occupied doing something constructive."

The same can go for your dog. Make a point of keeping him too busy to worry and obsess about his scary things.

You can even say that you are afraid of strange dogs. If you have a few "normal" dogs and are out walking them and people approach, you can start to educate them as to the proper etiquette for approaching or not approaching strange dogs. I do this all the time. You can get to know the clueless "regulars" in your area and avoid them either by walking in a different direction or going to that location at a different time of day. You should also be sure to practice the "come front," the "about turn" and some of the other quick getaway behaviors listed in Chapter Eight.

POINTS TO PONDER

❧ *Now you know the recipes and ingredients for the most wanted life-with-dog activities. Just remember, if you want to bake some bread and leave out the flour and yeast, it won't come out very palatable. Don't leave anything out in working with your dog, either.*

❧ *Plan your sessions carefully, always setting your dog up for success.*

❧ *Break your sessions down into tiny steps.*

❧ *Build on your foundation behaviors as well as other ones, keep your dog busy solving problems.*

❧ *Take it all slowly—don't expect to produce the perfect dog in a few weeks—or even months.*

The Golden Rules

THE PROCESS REVISITED

As you come to the conclusion of this book, the entire progression of systematic desensitization may seem daunting. It is and it isn't. The truth is, it is a simple process, but not an easy one. If you take it slow and look for progress in micro-steps, you will see improvement. Think of it in terms of scaling an enormous mountain. Instead of looking ahead and lamenting about how far you have yet to go, look behind you and rejoice in the progress you have already made. Set small and achievable goals. If your dog is continually aggressing, then you aren't making the steps small enough or going slow enough. It's that simple. There are a few rules to remember to keep you on track.

 Set your dog up to succeed.
Make it a fun game for you to stop the session before your dog aggresses. Don't think he isn't learning anything if the session is as short as fifteen seconds—he is. He is learning to practice calm behaviors, rather than aggressive ones.

 Teach your dog many alternate behaviors incompatible with aggressing.
The more positive, constructive behaviors he knows how to do, the less likely that he will aggress. Enrich his life and your own! He will learn that playing "games"with you is more rewarding for him than trying to chase away the scary stuff and much of his fear will dissipate.

Keep a log.

Keeping records is vital in the process to keep yourself on track. Review your sheets once a week, so you can see any good or bad trends and then be able to make any adjustments. Videotape your first session or two and thereafter once a month. We are human and, as humans, we tend to forget a great deal—this way, you can go back and watch the tapes and see just how much progress you have made. Always refer back to rule number one!

Set up your sessions carefully and completely.

Don't assume that your helpers know what to do. Spell it out exactly and make sure everyone knows what their "job" is. If your sessions are poorly planned out, then most likely they won't go as you wanted them to. This may seem very difficult at first, but the more you practice it, the easier it gets and the more "second nature" it becomes. Always refer back to rule number one!

The session starts when you have the leash in your hand and doesn't end until the dog is safely secured.

Watch your environment like a hawk! If you are aware of your dog and surroundings at all times, you won't miss the danger signs to get your dog back into safety. Neither will you miss the opportunities to reinforce good behavior. Always refer back to rule number one!

Make it fun for your dog to ignore his provoking stimuli.

Right now, your dog thinks the objects of his fear are things to repel with force. You need to change that mind-set and teach him that it is more fun and rewarding for him to ignore those previously scary things. Always refer back to rule number one!

Manage when you can't train.

There are times when management is the best solution at any given moment. For instance, if you have two dogs and usually walk them both together, change your strategy and walk them separately. You can't possibly pay attention and focus on your aggressive dog when you are walking both of them. If your dog is nervous about strangers coming to the house, then crate him when you have guests. If you aren't in the mood to work with your dog at any given time, then keep him safe! Always refer back to rule number one!

Keep it simple.

There really isn't anything mysterious or complicated about working with an aggressive dog. There are no magic wands, special pills, special equipment or gimmicks that will get you to your goal faster. It will take as long as it takes. Period. You will be amazed at how quickly your dog improves, just by keeping it simple and slow, following positive principles and systematic desensitization. Always refer back to rule number one!

Have goals.

Have short-term, mid-term and long-term goals. Short-term goals mark some kind of small progress in whatever your dog's issues are, such as calm attention from your dog while provoking stimuli are 300 feet away, his coming out of the car or house in a calm, focused manner or your dog allowing you to handle him for few seconds. A mid-term goal might be something like walking on a trail (with a helper) and having your dog focused on you or your dog allowing you to groom him thoroughly or building in reliability and generalization (focusing well in each and every new place). A long-term goal may be getting your Canine Good Citizen (CGC) certificate, competing in a dog sport or walking past a previously scary thing with no reaction whatsoever.

Your goals may include some of the behaviors listed in Chapter Ten—going through a toll booth, walking on a trail, allowing the vet to handle him, or having people or dogs walk past your yard—all without him aggressing.

Short term can mean as long as one year, or as little as five months. It all depends on you and your dog. Your short-, mid-, and long-term goals will change as your dog improves.

My first long-term goal with my dog Shadow was to get his CGC. Once that was achieved (it took eighteen months), my next long-term goal became walking him up to the front door of the supermarket (six months later) without me fainting or him aggressing. Competing in Rally obedience and agility came after that (approximately one year after his CGC). Now that those have been accomplished, my next long-term goal is to compete in competition obedience.

Be reasonable with your goals. Setting yourself up for success is as important as setting your dog up for success. By taking baby steps and achieving small goals, you will develop the desire, knowledge and tools to keep scaling the mountain towards your own personal summit.

COMPETITIVE SPORTS

There are actually many sports you can compete in (if that is what you aspire to) with a "recovering" aggressive dog. Even if you have no desire to compete, train for them anyway—they are quite fulfilling for both you and your dog. In the beginning, when training for these sports, please do not do a group class. This may be too much for your dog. Ask the instructor if you can have private lessons. If you sign up for a group class, you aren't following rule number one.

APDT Rally Obedience—a new and fun sport that is similar to competition obedience and agility. You follow a course of numbered signs and do the behaviors listed on each sign. The scoring is less stringent than competition obedience, and you can talk to your dog and even use food in the ring at certain stations. In level one, the dog is on leash at all times, there are no group stays, no stand for exam, and the judge stays far away from you while you do the course.

Karen and Xeres practicing Rally obedience. Photo by P. Dennison.

Agility—the speed obstacle course for dogs. This is a timed event and you need to run your dog through the course of obstacles accurately and safely.

Musical Freestyle—dancing with your dog to music. You are allowed to compete by videotape, so you can participate even before you are ready to go out in the "real" world.

Tracking—following a scent trail with a few direction changes to find a glove at the end. There are no other dogs or people on the field while you are running your dog, and your dog is on leash at all times.

Meg and Carly practicing Freestyle. Photo by J. Irizarry.

Sheepherding—any breed can train for this although only AKC sanctioned herding breeds can compete for titles.

Carting—you teach your dog to pull a cart. The competitions include certain behaviors—backing up, stays, walking across a "bridge," making right and left turns, etc.

Water Tests—there are different levels of classes you can train for. Some include swimming with your dog around buoys, having him do a stay while you swim out, and him jumping off a boat, retrieving objects, etc.

So you can see, even if your dog is aggressive, that doesn't mean he has to spend his entire life in the basement. He can learn to be calm and focused on you and then the sky's the limit. So what if he will never be a Therapy Dog? He won't know the difference.

Shadow with his training cart. Photo by P. Dennison.

Karen with her Rottweiler Gretchen during a water test. Photo by Three Dogs Running Studio for Animals Only.

Goals can include your own development as a trainer as well:

❧ Learning to be better with your timing

❧ Setting up your training sessions with more precision

❧ Learning how to stay focused on your dog and the task at hand

❧ Using more and varied reinforcement types with different and unpredictable reinforcement schedules

❧ Learning to read your dog's stress signals faster and with more accuracy

❧ Widening your horizons by learning how to teach more complicated behaviors

❧ Learning how to see progress in small increments

❧ Becoming completely calm in the presence of the things your dog used to be afraid of

Owning an aggressive dog is sometimes challenging, painful, emotionally draining and frustrating. There is no way to "rose color" these glasses. It takes a great deal of patience, fortitude, time, money and tissues to work with your dog long enough to see a real difference. If you let it, the thrill of overcoming your dog's issues will be one of the greatest experiences of your life.

Appendix 1

Training Lists and Forms

Please feel free to make copies of these pages. These lists may help you until being creative and unpredictable are as easy for you as breathing. Cut the suggestions into little strips and put them in a separate box marked for each kind of list (reinforcers, foundation behaviors and new behaviors). Pull a few slips out from each box for every training session—those are the behaviors you will practice and how you will reinforce them.

List of Suggested Reinforcers

Feel free to add in your own—be creative and watch your dog to see what floats his boat.

- A wad of treats, fed one at a time
- Throw food up in the air while cheering
- Clap
- Cheer
- Soft petting
- Rough petting
- Blow bubbles
- Go sniff
- Sniff the food
- Tease with toy

❖ Play with toy
❖ Pluck grass or snow and throw it up in the air
❖ Run around silly
❖ Go swimming
❖ Nose target your hand
❖ The chance to do a favorite pet trick
❖ Play with a special friend (human or dog)

List of Foundation Behaviors
A few of these should be practiced at each training session.

❖ Bridge response
❖ Eye contact
❖ Name recognition
❖ Heel on loose leash
❖ Accept touch
❖ Accept secondary reinforcers
❖ Stays
❖ Come (recall)
❖ Door etiquette
❖ Trading (not being possessive about objects/people/locations)
❖ Crate training

List of New Behaviors to Train During a Training/Desensitization Session
Pick one or two per session. If the behavior is very complicated, then only pick one to train at a time.

❖ Retrieve an object
❖ Jump through a hula hoop or over a jump
❖ Moving stand
❖ Sit
❖ Down

- Stay
- Shake paw
- Hand signals for sit and down
- Spin to the right and left
- Weave in between your legs
- "Clean up" (put toys in basket on cue)
- Roll over
- Settle
- Bow
- Agility obstacles (tire, table, tunnel, weaves, teeter, A-frame, dog walk, chute, jumps)
- Ride a skateboard
- Balance on a board with a tennis ball nailed to the bottom
- Track (find the person whose scent "pad" he has sniffed or even just follow a scent of liver that you dragged along the ground)
- "Wipe your feet" (on a towel or mat)
- Wag tail on cue
- Close a door
- Ring a bell
- Pick out a sock that has your scent on it from a pile of otherwise clean socks
- Find your keys
- Automatic sits with continued focus when you stop moving
- Right turns and left turns
- About turns
- Stand for exam (on ground or on table)
- Drop on recall
- Drop as he is running away from you
- Call front
- Instant down
- Fast and slow pace
- Directionals

- Come away from the other dogs in your household
- Accept muzzle
- "Go visit"
- Nose target your hand
- Find a treat or toy under a towel or blanket

LOG SHEETS
Sample Training Log

Date: _5/10/04_   Location: _Walking on the trail_

Context: (describe in detail)_ One person and dog in front of us and one person and dog behind us, both at a 30-foot distance_

Number of minutes:_ 10 minutes—5 minutes out and 5 minutes back_

Rate the behaviors practiced from 1-5, 5 being great:

_3_ eye contact _5_ name recognition _3_ heeling on loose leash _5_ recall _5_ sit _5_ down _X_ stay _4_ basic attention _5_ door etiquette _5_ crate training _2_ accept touch

__other behaviors (describe)_ threw a toy and played fetch_

Reinforcers used: _Food, petting, pet tricks, toss the stick_

Any reaction? Describe in detail: _His door etiquette coming out of the van was perfect. From the van to the trail, I let him get ahead of me by a few feet and practiced calling him back. He was successful each time (4 times). Lots of good smells today and his attention could have been better. He kept looking back at the person and dog following us in a sort of nervous way, but there was no aggressive reaction. There was a jogger that went by, so we ran off into the woods and I fed him while the jogger passed. I tried to use petting as a reinforcer, but sometimes he avoided it._

Note: X means we didn't practice that behavior.

TRAINING LOG

Date:_____ Location:_____

Context: (describe in detail)_____

_____

_____

_____

_____

Number of minutes:_____

Rate the behaviors practiced from 1-5, 5 being great:

___eye contact ___name recognition ___heeling on loose leash ___recall

___ sit ___down ___stay ___basic attention ___door etiquette ___crate

training ___accept touch

__other behaviors (describe)_____

_____

Reinforcers used: _____

Any reaction? Describe in detail: _____

_____

_____

_____

_____

_____

_____

_____

_____

LOG SHEET FOR YOUR HELPER

This is a great way to evaluate how your sessions are going. It is often very hard to remember exactly what you did during a session because you were so busy trying not to hyperventilate. It is valuable to have someone watch and record for you the answers to the following questions.

HOW MANY DIFFERENT BEHAVIORS DID YOU SEE?

What were they?_____

Did you see any foundation behaviors being practiced?_____

What were they?_____

Did you see any new behaviors being practiced?_____

What were they?_____

How many different types of reinforcers did you see used?_____

What were they?_____

Did you see any calming/stress signals?_____

What were they?_____

Did you see any progress in the session?_____

What was it?_____

What needs work?_____

Breakdown of My Dog's Issues

This sheet should be filled out at the beginning of your training and then again every six months to go along with your log sheets. Knowing exactly what triggers your dog to react or aggress is the first step in helping him. This will help you see progress and what you still need to work on. If you need more room or have different issues than listed below, add to the bottom of the form. Be sure to keep it simple and make it easy on yourself—you don't need full sentences. Be sure to define the distance for each of these things as well as duration (how long your dog can be in the presence of the stimulus before aggressing).

MY DOG'S ISSUES

Date:_____

Things my dog aggresses at: ___Men ___Women ___Kids (define—ages, walking, running, on bikes or skateboards, swimming, playing)_____

___Men in hats ___Men with beards ___One person alone

___Groups of people ___ Eye contact from strangers

___Moving body parts ___Direct contact

___Grooming (define) _____

___ People walking ___ People running/jogging

___ People coming up from behind ___ Mail or UPS person

___ People on the other side of a fence or barrier

Other _____

___Direct eye contact from a dog

___Certain breed(s) of dogs (list)_____

___Male dogs (intact/neutered) ___Female dogs (intact/spayed)

___Dogs running ___Dogs walking ___Dogs playing ___Dogs coming up to the crate ___Dogs approaching head on ___Dogs sniffing his hind end ___On leash __Off leash ___Puppies

Other_____

Inanimate objects: ___Coats ___Sunglasses ___Hats ___Gloves ___Boots

___Umbrellas ___Playground equipment ___Stuffed animals

___Drainpipes ___Manhole covers ___Papers blowing in the wind

___Loud noises ___Trucks ___Water (bath, lake or river) ___Gravel

___Ice ___Pots and pans dropping ___Thunder___Shopping carts

___Loud music

Other_____

Appendix 2

Additional Resources

READING LIST

Training

Bones Would Rain From the Sky, by Suzanne Clothier
Bringing Light to Shadow: A Dog Trainer's Diary, by Pamela Dennison
Calming Signals, On Talking Terms with Dogs (video and book), by Turid
    Rugaas
Clicker Training for Obedience: Shaping Top Performance Positively (for
    competition), by Morgan Spector
Coercion and Its Fallout, by Murray Sidman
The Complete Idiot's Guide to Positive Dog Training, by Pamela Dennison
Conquering Ring Nerves: A Step-by-Step Program for All Dog Sports, by
    Diane Peters Mayer, MSW
Culture Clash, by Jean Donaldson
Excel-erated Learning, by Pamela Reid
How Dogs Learn, by Mary Burch and Jon Baily
Learning and Behavior, by Paul Chance
Mine, by Jean Donaldson
On Aggression, by Konrad Lorenz
The Other End of the Leash, by Patricia McConnell
That Winning Feeling, by Jane Savoie
Why Zebras Don't Get Ulcers, by Robert Sapolsky

Health

The Holistic Guide for a Healthy Dog, by Wendy Volhard and Kerry Brown
Dr. Pitcairn's Complete Guide to Natural Health for Dogs and Cats, by
    Richard H. Pitcairn and Susan Hubble Pitcairn
Give Your Dog a Bone or Grow Your Pups with Bones, by Ian Billinghurst

WEBSITES

General Book Resources—sites where you can order the books listed above

www.dogwise.com

www.amazon.com

www.sitstay.com

Health

http://www.truthaboutvaccines.org/

Thyroid Information

    Dr. Jean Dodds has been the forerunner in thyroid information in dogs. A complete thyroid panel should be run, including total thyroxine (TT4), total TT3, free T4, free T3, T4 autoantibody, T3 autoantibody, thyroid stimulating hormone and thryroglobulin autoantibody. The best lab to send the blood to is Michigan State University, which has the most experience in properly reading the results. For more information about Dr. Dodds, simply search online using her name. For information on sending blood, go to: http://www.itsfortheanimals.com/HEMOPET.HTM

Behavior and Training—sites where you can learn more about behavior and training

http://www.dogexpert.com/Polsky%20Papers/Electronicfences.html

http://www.wagntrain.com/OC/

http://employees.csbsju.edu/tcreed/pb/operant.html

http://employees.csbsju.edu/tcreed/pb/pavcon.html

http://www.flyingdogpress.com/

http://www.vin.com/VINDBPub/SearchPB/Proceedings/PR05000/PR00312
    .htm

http://www.bcrescuetexas.org/Training/DESENSITIZATION

http://www.mentalhelp.net/psyhelp/chap12/chap12g.htm

Finding a Trainer

Be careful to interview the instructor carefully and if there is anything you don't agree with, then keep shopping around. Not everyone has the same expertise in working with aggression and you will find many trainers that still think punishment is the best way to deal with it.

Association of Pet Dog Trainers
www.apdt.com

National Association of Dog Obedience Instructors
www.nadoi.org

Pos-4-Reactive dogs e-mail list
www.Pos-4-ReactiveDogs@yahoogroups.com

Dog Sports

Most of these sites have e-mail lists for you to join and learn about the ins and outs of each sport.

APDT Rally Obedience
www.apdt.com

Freestyle
www.worldcaninefreestyle.org
www.canine-freestyle.org

Tracking
www.akc.org
You may also search online for "tracking."

Water work
www.caninewatersports.com

Carting
Carting-L@yahoogroups.com

Agility
NADAC (North American Dog Agility Council)
www.nadac.com

AKC
www.akc.org

USDAA (United States Dog Agility Association)
www.usdaa.com

Miscellaneous

Pam Dennison—*Information on training, health, vaccination protocols, car sickness info, skunk remedies, recipes and Camp R.E.W.A.R.D. for aggressive dogs.*
www.positivedogs.com

Tellington TTouch—*Information about the Tellington TTouch*
http://www.lindatellingtonjones.com/ttouch.shtml

Clicker Solutions—*A great resource for articles*
http://www.clickersolutions.com/index.html

Stacy Braslau-Schneck—*Another great source for articles*
http://www.wagntrain.com/OC/

Competing at Your Peak—*For performance anxiety*
www.competingatyourpeak.com

TRAINING TOOLS

I am sure you noticed in this book that I don't mention "tools" other than a flat buckle collar or harness and a long line. The following are my favorite places to get these things:

Black Ice Dog Sledding
The X back sledding harness (item #HS52)—www.blackice-dogsledding.com. Phone: 320-485-4825. Go to their website and look for the instructions on how to measure for a harness. Measure TWICE, order once. This harness is not adjustable.

Lawson K9

> ***Leather tracking harness*** (item #LTS250)—www.lawsonk9.com. Phone: 336-407-7088. This is my other pick for a harness. Use this if your dog tends to back out of collars or if he is the size of a big Lab or German Shepherd. He won't be able to get out of this tracking harness. The harnesses are beautifully made, comfortable and fully adjustable, and they ship quickly. Click on the harness section (by all means, ignore the prong collars and other icky stuff on the site) and scroll down to item LTS250. Get the single-ply harness—most dogs fit into the medium size one. This harness is fully adjustable.

Bridgeport Equipment

> ***Leashes***—www.bridgeportequipment.com. Phone: 1-800-678-7353 or 614-864-0336. This company has the best leashes. For the 33-foot long lines (leather and nylon) go to the tracking section. I use the 3/8" or the 1/2" wide. When buying a long line, don't get cotton—they rot and break at the worst possible moment!

Glossary

Antecedents or Cues—anything that comes *before* a behavior, e.g., a can opener, a hand signal or verbal cue or the appearance of a strange dog or person.

Avoidance—the behavior prevents an impending unpleasant circumstance.

Behaviors—the actions that are motivated by the cue; what the dog does, be it a sit, down or whatever.

Classical conditioning—when something that has no particular meaning for the dog *(a neutral stimulus)*, such as a tone or light, becomes paired with something that does have meaning for the dog, such as food or water, physical pain or pleasure.

Consequences—what happens to the dog as a direct result of performing the behavior.

Context—the whole situation, including what is happening in the environment, how long the sessions last, what you and your dog are doing, plus every other detail in each specific session.

Counterconditioning—works to replace bad or unpleasant emotional responses (due to prior conditioning)—hence the word, *counter*—to a stimulus with more pleasant responses.

Desensitization or Systematic desensitization—a procedure in which the dog is exposed to extremely low levels (distance, duration) of a frightening stimulus while great things (the best food, toys, play, petting, praise) are happening to him (while he is calm). The level of the frightening stimulus is gradually increased, but never at a rate to cause distress.

Escape—the behavior lessens the existing aversiveness.

Fixed interval reinforcement—reinforcing after the same amount of time elapsed—every five seconds for example.

Fixed ratio reinforcement—reinforcing after the same amounts of behaviors—for instance, after every third sit.

Flooding—a prolonged and forced exposure to stimulus that is or has become noxious (terrifying or frightening).

Negative punishment (-P)—anything taken away (negative) *(that your dog likes)* that decreases (punishes) behavior.

Negative reinforcement (-R)—anything taken away (negative) *(that your dog doesn't like)* that increases (reinforces) behavior.

Operant conditioning—Operant behavior is voluntary behavior that is influenced by its consequences. Those consequences may increase or decrease behavior. Operant conditioning is broken down to antecedent, behavior and consequence.

Positive punishment (+P)—anything added (positive) *(that your dog doesn't like)* that decreases (punishes) behavior.

Positive reinforcement(+R)—anything added (positive) *(that your dog likes)* that increases (reinforces) behavior.

Primary reinforcers—food, water and access to sex.

Provoking stimuli—things that provoke your dog into an aggressive display.

Secondary reinforcers—touch, toys, praise, play, or anything else you can think up.

Stimuli, stimulus—something that triggers the dog to react in a specific way.

Variable interval reinforcement—reinforcing after different amounts of time elapsed—after five seconds, twelve seconds, twenty seconds, three seconds, eight seconds, etc.

Variable ratio reinforcement—reinforcing after different amounts of behaviors—for instance, after one sit, ten sits, three sits, nine sits, etc.

About the Author

Pam Dennison's work with aggressive dogs started when she adopted a one-year-old Border Collie named Shadow. Unbeknownst to her, she had a human-aggressive dog on her hands. It was through her work with Shadow and mentoring with Carolyn Wilki and Ted Turner (the nationally known animal behaviorist) that she was able to gain the observational and training skills necessary to work with aggressive dogs. In a mere eighteen months, Pam took Shadow from being a human-aggressive dog to one able to earn his Canine Good Citizen certificate. Based on her work with Shadow, Pam now holds behavior modification classes for aggressive and reactive dogs, as well as seminars and camps (Camp R.E.W.A.R.D.)

Pam has been training dogs since 1992 and started her own business, Positive Motivation Dog Training, in 1997. She teaches puppy kindergarten, beginners, Canine Good Citizen, musical Freestyle, Rally and competition classes at her facility in Blairstown, New Jersey. Pam works with every breed, from Dachshunds to Great Danes to every size in between, on a myriad of behavioral issues.

Pam started competing in 1996 and qualified and competed in the Eastern United States Dog Obedience Championships in 1997. After switching to positive training methods from traditional, punishment-based ones, she started her own school in 1997. At present she lives with three rescued dogs (two Border Collies and one Shetland Sheepdog). Her dogs have earned many titles to date, encompassing Competition obedience, Rally obedience, and agility. Pam continues to compete for more titles in these sports, as well as training for sheepherding, tracking, carting, and water sports. To date, her students have earned a multitude of titles and certificates in obedience, Rally, tracking, sheepherding and Canine Good Citizen and Therapy Dog programs.

Pam is the author of *The Complete Idiot's Guide to Positive Dog Training* (Alpha Books) and *Bringing Light to Shadow: A Dog Trainer's Diary* (Dogwise Publishing). Pam also has two videos available, *Camp R.E.W.A.R.D. for Aggressive Dogs,* and *Positive Solutions for Standard*

185

Behavioral Problems, both from Barkleigh Productions. Pam is a member of the APDT (Association of Pet Dog Trainers), the NADOI (National Association of Dog Obedience Instructors) and the DWAA (Dog Writers Association of America), and is a Certified Animal Behavior Consultant with the IAABC (International Association of Animal Behavior Consultants).

Pam has published articles in the *Blairstown Press* and *The Clicker Journal* and is the training editor for the New England Border Collie Rescue newsletter, *Have You Herd?* She was a regular guest speaker on *Wednesday in the Doghouse,* 1360 AM WNJC, a Philadelphia radio show hosted by Renee Premaza, and has appeared at various dog training clubs, Therapy Dog groups, the Off Lead Training Expo, and GlaxoSmithKline, speaking on a variety of topics relating to positive training and aggression. Pam also has worked closely with Sussex County Friends of Animals, where she developed a retraining program for shelter dogs.

Index

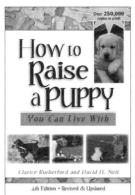

ORDER YOUR COPY TODAY!

❏ **YES!** I want to order ___ copies of *How to Right a Dog Gone Wrong* at U.S. $19.95 each plus $6 shipping per book. (Colorado residents please add 3% tax). Canadian orders must be accompanied by a postal money order in U.S funds. *Please allow 15 days for delivery.*

My ❏ check or ❏ money order for $_____ is enclosed.

❏ Please charge my: ❏ VISA ❏ MasterCard

Credit #_____ exp date_____

Deliver to:

Name _____

Organization _____

Address _____

City _____State _____Zip _____

Phone _____ email _____

❏ Please send information on how I can earn **FREE BOOKS** by referring *How to Right a Dog Gone Wrong* to others!

Breeders • Clubs • Organizations • CALL FOR DISCOUNTS!

Mail to: Alpine Publications, P.O. Box 7027, Loveland, CO 80537

CALL 1-800-777-7257 • E-MAIL alpinecsr@aol.com

Browse all our titles at: ***www.alpinepub.com***